SURRENDER

The Heart God Controls

SURRENDER
The Heart God Controls

NANCY LEIGH DEMOSS

Revive Our Hearts

MOODY PUBLISHERS
CHICAGO

Editor: Cheryl Dunlop
Interior Design: BlueFrog Design
Cover Design: Smartt Guys design
Cover Photo: Douglas E. Walker/Masterfile

Library of Congress Cataloging-in-Publication Data

DeMoss, Nancy Leigh.
   Surrender : the heart God controls / Nancy Leigh DeMoss.
     p. cm.
   Includes bibliographical references.
   ISBN 13: 978-0-8024-1280-5
   1. Christian life. 2. Spiritual warfare. I. Title.
 BV4501.3.D45 2003
 248.4--dc21

                                                        2003007130

We hope you enjoy this book from Moody Publishers. Our goal is to provide high-quality, thought-provoking books and products that connect truth to your real needs and challenges. For more information on other books and products written and produced from a biblical perspective, go to www.moodypublishers.com or write to:
Moody Publishers
820 N. LaSalle Boulevard
Chicago, IL 60610

9 10

Printed in the United States of America

O God whose will conquers all,
There is no comfort in anything
    apart from enjoying thee
    and being engaged in thy service;
Thou art All in all, and all enjoyments are what to me
    thou makest them, and no more.
I am well pleased with thy will, whatever it is,
    or should be in all respects,
And if thou bidst me decide for myself in any affair
    I would choose to refer all to thee,
    for thou art infinitely wise and cannot do amiss,
    as I am in danger of doing.
I rejoice to think that all things are at thy disposal,
    and it delights me to leave them there. . . .
I can of myself do nothing to glorify thy blessed name,
    but I can through grace cheerfully surrender soul
    and body to thee.

—From *The Valley of Vision: A Collection of
Puritan Prayers and Devotion*

CONTENTS

FOREWORD

I will never forget that special visit to Lima, Peru. I was on my way to preach in Argentina but stopped for a few days to attend the annual conference of a national movement of churches dedicated to spreading the gospel of Christ throughout all of Peru.

The service that evening was a blessing, even though I had to depend greatly on an interpreter sitting next to me. In the middle of the meeting, the leadership called to the platform a young couple who seemed to be in their late twenties. As the leaders introduced them to the audience and prepared to pray for them, the congregation began singing a beautiful Spanish chorus of worship to the Lord.

Suddenly, the presence of the Lord descended on that service in a palpable and fresh way. I turned to my friend and asked what exactly was going on. It turned out the young couple had been trained to minister God's Word and were leaving after much prayer to pioneer a church in a remote jungle area in Peru. I learned later that they had no church building or congregation waiting for them, nor a home prepared to live in.

With only the few dollars the conference gave them, this man and his wife were stepping out in faith and total surrender to God's purpose for their lives. A hundred and one things we might worry about were as nothing to them. I still remember their shining faces and the tears of joy in their eyes. I also can never forget how God melted and ministered to my own heart through their surrender to Jesus.

The highest possible worship and service to God is when we obey the apostle Paul's plea in Romans 12:1 (NIV, italics added): "Therefore, I urge you, brothers, in view of God's mercy, to *offer your bodies as living sacrifices,* holy and pleasing to God—*this* is your spiritual act of worship."

Christianity without this principle of heart surrender to our living Lord is a contradiction of the very essence of following Jesus. It produces spiritually bankrupt lives and churches that are listless and impotent. It does require grace to sing "Hallelujah" to God, but far more grace is needed to sincerely sing "I Surrender All."

Many years ago, a young Methodist minister was struggling with his calling and a severe attack of discouragement. He was hoping his assignment from God might change, but his superiors reappointed him to the same difficult place of ministry. As the spiritual crisis deepened within him, he came to the breaking point of *surrender to God's will* no matter what that might mean. That day, he also wrote a hymn that is one of the first I remember hearing in church as a child:

> *Would you have Him make you free,*
> *And follow at His call?*
> *Would you know the peace*
> *That comes by giving all?*
> *Would you have Him save you*
> *So that you can never fall?*
> *Let Him have His way with thee.*
>
> *His power can make you what you ought to be,*
> *His blood can cleanse your heart*
> *And make you free,*
> *His love can fill your soul,*
> *And you will see*
> *'Twas best for Him to have His way with thee.*

—"His Way With Thee," C. S. Nusbaum

I am so happy that Nancy Leigh DeMoss has written this powerful book on surrender to God and its implications for each of us and the kingdom of God. May the Lord use it around the world for His glory!

—Jim Cymbala, Senior Pastor
The Brooklyn Tabernacle

ACKNOWLEDGMENTS

Like all new births, every book has its own gestation, labor, and delivery process, with a variety of professionals and friends supporting and assisting along the way. This book is no exception. I owe special thanks to . . .

- *My friends at Moody Publishers*—you are kindred spirits and true partners in ministry.

- *Lela Gilbert* for your input during the developmental stage and for your contribution to parts of chapter 5, in particular.

- *Carolyn McCulley* for your valuable help with the initial shaping of the discussion guide.

❋ *Holly Elliff, Andrea Griffith, Tim Grissom,* and *Dr. Bill Thrasher* for reading various drafts and offering helpful suggestions.

❋ The wonderful men and women who serve on the staff of *Revive Our Hearts.* I am especially grateful to *Dawn Wilson* for your research assistance and to *Mike Neises* for your godly, wise management of our publishing efforts.

❋ *Dr. Bruce Ware* for the safeguard of your careful theological review.

❋ *Bob Lepine* for your help in developing, shaping, and refining this message. Your contribution has been substantial and invaluable.

❋ *My "praying friends"*—you'll never know this side of eternity how much I need and count on your prayers and encouragement. You have helped me stay the course and have made me a far more fruitful servant than I ever could have been without you.

INTRODUCTION

*There will likely be a time in our
Christian journeys when, like
Jacob, we will wrestle with God all
night long. . . . But there must
eventually come a dawn when we
say, "OK, God, You win. . . . Not
my will but Thine be done."*

GARY THOMAS[1]

On March 10, 1974, almost thirty years after the end of World War II, Lt. Hiroo Onoda finally handed over his rusty sword and became the last Japanese soldier to surrender.

Onoda had been sent to the tropical island of Lubang in the Philippines in 1944, with orders to conduct guerrilla warfare and prevent enemy attack on the island. When the war ended, Onoda refused to believe the messages announcing Japan's surrender.

For twenty-nine years, long after all his fellow soldiers had either surrendered or been killed off, Onoda continued defending the island territory for the defeated Japanese army. He hid in the jungle, living off the land, stealing food and supplies from local citizens, evading one search party after another, and killing at least thirty nationals in the process. Hundreds of thousands of dollars were spent trying to locate the lone holdout and convince him that the war was over.

Leaflets, newspapers, photographs, and letters from friends were dropped in the jungle; announcements were made over loudspeakers, begging Onoda to surrender. Still he refused to give up his fight. Some thirteen thousand men had been deployed in the effort before Onoda finally received a personal command from his former commander and was persuaded to give up the futile, solitary war he had waged for so many years.[2]

In his autobiography entitled, *No Surrender: My Thirty-Year War,* Onoda describes the moment that the reality of what had transpired began to sink in:

> I felt like a fool. . . . What had I been doing for all these years? . . . For the first time I really understood. . . . This was the end. I pulled back the bolt on my rifle and unloaded the bullets. . . . I eased off the pack that I always carried with me and laid the gun on top of it.[3]

The war was finally over.

Our Personal War

From our vantage point today, Hiroo Onoda seems to have been sadly mistaken at best, absurdly foolish at worst. The best years of his life—thrown away, fighting a war whose outcome had already been determined.

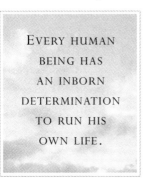

EVERY HUMAN BEING HAS AN INBORN DETERMINATION TO RUN HIS OWN LIFE.

Yet, in a sense, Onoda's story isn't unique to him. It's our story as well. We all begin life as members of a rebellious race, fighting our own personal war against the Sovereign King of the universe. For most, that resistance unfolds into a lifelong story that could be titled *No Surrender.*

Some express their resistance overtly, perhaps through a lifestyle of unbridled lust and perversion. Others are more subtle—they are upstanding citizens and community leaders; they may even be active in church work. But beneath the surface, every human being has an inborn determination to run his own life and an unwillingness to be mastered by Christ, the King of Kings.

The decision to give up the fight is no small matter, especially after years of resistance. In Onoda's case, he had become accustomed to living as a lone guerilla soldier, moving from one jungle hideout to another, dodging all attempts to subdue him. By the time he was fifty-two years old, he scarcely knew any other way to live. Resisting, running, and hiding had become the *norm*—the way of life with which he was most familiar and comfortable. For Onoda, surrender meant nothing less than a radically altered lifestyle.

IT'S TIME TO HAND OVER YOUR SWORD.

Surrender to Christ as Savior and Lord is no less life-changing. Whether we first wave the white flag at the age of eight or eighty-eight, that surrender involves a transfer of allegiance and a transformation of perspective that ought to affect every aspect of our lives.

I assume that most who are reading this book have come to that initial point of surrender that the Bible identifies as being born again: You have placed your faith in Christ's sacrifice for your sin, relinquished control of your life to Him, and been converted into the kingdom (the control) of God. My hope is that you will grow in your understanding of what it means to live out the implications of that surrender on a daily basis.

I have no doubt, however, that some who are reading these words have never come to that point: You may have made a profession of faith; you may have long considered yourself a Christian, and others may assume that you are a Christian, but you

20

have never truly been born into the family of God—
you have never waved the white flag of surrender to
Christ; you have never relinquished the right to run
your own life.

My appeal to you is to recognize the foolishness
and futility of further resistance and to believe and
obey the gospel that *Jesus is Lord. The war is over . . .*
it's time to hand over your sword to the King of Kings!

A Lifetime of Surrender

You may be thinking, *I gave my life to Christ years
ago; tell me something new.*

Here's what's new for many. That initial surrender
to Christ (which we often refer to as the point of salvation) was not the end of the story. In fact, it was
really the starting place.

That point of surrender simply set the stage for a
lifetime of surrender. Having surrendered our lives to
Christ as Savior and Lord, we must now learn what
it means to live out a surrendered life—to contin-
ually say *no* to self and *yes* to God.

Many Christians live perpetually discouraged,
defeated lives because they have never realized (and
therefore are not living out) the implications of their
initial surrender to Christ. Having once surrendered
control of their lives to Christ, they have reverted to
trying to manage their own lives. As a result, they are

living out of alignment with the Lord who created, redeemed, and owns them.

It may be that even at this moment you are living in a chapter called "Unsurrendered." Oh, that may not describe your whole way of life—you can probably point to specific areas where you are obeying God. But could it be that there are some issues on which you are reserving the right to control your own life?

REASONS FOR LACK OF SURRENDER

At certain points in their journey, those who have professed faith in Christ may find themselves "unsurrendered" to God's control in particular areas of their lives. The reasons for this may vary.

For example, though they may have truly surrendered their lives to God, they may have never realized some of the specific implications of that surrender— *You mean, my money belongs to God? My kids? My body? My time? I'd never thought about that!* As you read the pages that follow, I pray God will open your eyes to see the practical outworking of a surrendered life in ways you may never have considered.

In some cases, believers know what it means to live under God's control, but they are afraid of what might happen if they surrender some particular area—*If I surrender my family to the Lord, what will happen to them? If I surrender my finances, will my needs be met?* If you are wrestling with fears about the will of God, I want to encourage you with the promises of God and to help you understand that He is worthy of all your trust.

In a third scenario, some people claim to be surrendered to God, and may even believe that they are, but (perhaps subconsciously) they are justifying and rationalizing certain habits, values, attitudes, or behaviors that are contrary to the Word of God. *What about the stuff I watch on movies and TV? I don't think it's really that bad. OK, I admit I have a chronic struggle with overeating and with controlling my temper. But I'm just human. None of us is going to be perfect until we get to heaven.*

To some extent, we all find ourselves in this "deceived" condition at times. We so easily become desensitized to God's standards or feel that compared to the world's standards we are doing fine.

In fact, writing this book has forced me to face a number of matters in my own life that I had been overlooking, tolerating, or excusing that are really "surrender issues" at heart.

If you claim to be a follower of Christ while living in denial about certain areas of your life that are not pleasing to Him, my desire is to help you see the truth—that you are not living a fully surrendered life, no matter how many people may think of you as a "good Christian." (A word of caution here: If, over a period of time, you continue to be deceived and are unwilling or unable to acknowledge the truth, it may well be that your *profession* of faith falls short of *true* belief.)

Finally, some professing believers are living in willful rebellion against God's control in specific areas of their lives—*I know what God wants me to do, but I'm just not going to obey.* If that is true of your life, you are in one of two dangerous conditions:

(1) You are not really a Christian—you are deceiving yourself and others about the true state of your soul, and you are living under the wrath of God and facing eternal judgment, despite any profession of faith you may have made (Matthew 7:21–23); or

(2) You are a rebellious child of God, and you can expect to experience the loving correction and discipline of God until you repent or until God ends your life (1 Corinthians 11:27–32; Hebrews 12:6).

Either way, the consequences of persisting in willful rebellion are severe. To live in conscious resistance against God is no trivial matter. In fact, if that characterizes your lifestyle, it is likely you have never truly been born again. At best, you have no basis for claiming to be a child of God or for having assurance of salvation.

Genuine saving faith is always accompanied by repentance and must be followed by ongoing growth in obeying God (2 Peter 1:4–8); that does not mean perfect obedience, to be sure, but a desire to move from rebellion toward greater surrender to and satisfaction in God.

Whatever the reason for your lack of surrender (whether in isolated issues or as a way of life), you may have settled into that lifestyle for so long that you don't know any other way to live. Maybe you even think this is *normal*—after all, your life may not be so different from lots of other people you know. In fact, compared to many other professing Christians, you may seem like a spiritual giant.

However, regardless of what seems to be typical, *the fully surrendered life is intended to be—and can be —the norm for every one of God's children.*

THE HIGH PRICE OF HOLDING OUT

Do you fear what a lifestyle of full surrender might cost you? Then consider the cost of holding out on God. I think of professing believers I know who have tragically wasted what could have been the most productive, fruitful years of their lives, much as Hiroo Onoda did. They have been satisfied to fend for themselves and forage off the land when they could have been feasting at His banquet table.

They have settled for wartime conditions when they could have been enjoying the blessings of peace.

As was true in Onoda's case, others' lives are invariably affected by our resistance. I have watched men and women whose refusal to surrender has left a trail of broken relationships—with parents, mate, children, friends, fellow church members, and others.

Onoda might understandably have feared the consequences he would face if he were to surrender. Would he be tried as a war criminal? Might he be sentenced to death? Imagine Onoda's relief when he finally turned over his sword and surrendered to President Marcos of the Philippines, and the president immediately issued him a full and complete pardon.

The truth is that resistance is far more costly than surrender. To reject God's gracious provision of salvation and to refuse His command to repent means eternal punishment for sin. For those of us who are followers of Christ, any resistance to the will of God will keep us from enjoying an abundant life and will create barriers in our fellowship with God.

But our God abounds in mercy and grace; He is willing to offer a full and complete pardon to those who lay down their weapons.

In eternity, knowing what we cannot see now or what we have refused to believe, any holding out on our part will appear no less misguided and foolish than a Japanese officer spending three decades of his adult life holed up in a tropical jungle, living like an animal, fighting a war that had long since ended.

As we consider the meaning of Christian surrender, I pray that your heart will be captured with a compelling vision of the One who claims the right to run the universe. May you experience an irresistible sense of the joys and blessings that can be yours through relinquishing control to this God who loves you and who holds your very life in His hand.

Notes

1. Gary Thomas, *Seeking The Face of God* (Eugene, Oreg.: Harvest House, 1999), 84.
2. "Old Soldiers Never Die," *Newsweek,* March 25, 1974, 49, 52.
3. Hiroo Onoda, *No Surrender: My Thirty-Year War* (New York: Kodansha International Ltd., 1974), 14–15.

CHAPTER 1

THE BATTLE FOR CONTROL:
KINGDOMS AT WAR

*Surrender is not the surrender of
the external life, but of the will;
when that is done, all is done.
There are very few crises in life;
the great crisis is
the surrender of the will.*

❄

OSWALD CHAMBERS[1]

❄

✸ **Mindy,** a Christian college senior, can't believe she ended up in bed with her fiancé last night—again—after promising herself she wouldn't give in and praying about the matter with her accountability partner just last week. Mindy and Jeff are planning to get married after graduation and had hoped to serve as short-term missionaries before having children. But now . . . the whole idea seems hypocritical.

✸ Angie steps on the scales, sighs, and heads for the kitchen, where she opens the refrigerator. She starts to pick up a bag of carrots, then reaches instead for a piece of carrot cake that seems to be calling her name. Just then, the phone rings; her sister is calling to offer a ride to their weekly Bible class tomorrow morning.

* Something inside Dan knows he really shouldn't be going out for "business lunches" with his attractive young assistant—especially since their recent conversations have been less about business and more about the problems in her marriage. Dan is nervous about being seen with Stacie by someone from the church where he is a respected elder. But some unseen force is drawing him to spend more time with her.

* Both Tamara and Rod would like for her to be able to quit her job so she can stay at home when their first child is born next month, but they just don't see how they can swing it financially. Their pastor recently preached a message from Matthew 6 about trusting God to provide for basic needs. But they are afraid to step out—and his parents have said she'd be crazy to quit her job.

* Reggie is still fuming as he flies down the freeway at eighty miles per hour. He knows he shouldn't have lost his temper with Carla—especially with their three-year-old son standing there watching the whole scene. But he can't believe she has overdrawn their checking account again. Why can't she exer-

cise some self-control when it comes to spending? Reggie gets scared when he thinks about what he might do someday when he is in one of his fits of rage. Recently his anger has started coming out with the students at the Christian school where he coaches football.

✸ Corrie is troubled by the attitudes and language her children are picking up from other children in preschool and second grade. She wants her children to have a heart for God and really feels she should consider homeschooling them, but she can't handle the thought of being tied down with kids all day every day.

THE REAL WAR

These men and women are not alone in their struggles. Every day, in big or little ways, even as believers, you and I find ourselves engaged in a battle (Galatians 5:17).

The battle is real and dangerous. We are like a soldier in a foxhole, with bullets whizzing past his head, but our battle is actually part of a larger war that has been going on since the creation of the world.

In fact, one of the megathemes that emerges repeatedly in Scripture is that our battles here on earth are merely a reflection of a cosmic war between the kingdom of God and all other kingdoms. That is true whether we are talking about kids squabbling on a playground, embattled parents and teens, estranged mates in a divorce court, warring desires within our own hearts, power struggles in the church, or nations at war.

This bigger war—the "real war"—begins in the opening pages of the Word of God and continues unabated, gaining in intensity, almost to the final page. It is, in essence, a battle for control.

In the first recorded act in time and space, God *exercised control.* He spoke with authority and power . . . bringing light, life, and order to the darkness and chaos of the universe. When He said, "Let there be light," there was light. When He said, "Let the trees bring forth fruit," the trees brought forth fruit. All creation, including—initially—the first man and woman, lived in glad, wholehearted surrender to the sovereign control and will of the Creator.

This surrender did not strip the creation of dignity or freedom; to the contrary, surrender was—and still is—the source and means of true freedom and fullness. The sovereign Creator God ruled over His creation with tender love, inviting His creatures to engage with Him in a divine dance-of-sorts, in which He led and they followed. They responded to His initiative with trust, love, and surrender. In turn, their needs were abundantly met, they fulfilled their created purpose, and they existed in harmony with God and with each other.

Psalm 104 describes this original, ideal state. In that passage, we see a definite, unquestioned hierarchy in which God—the gracious Sovereign—acts, initiates, directs, sets boundaries, supervises, and lovingly rules over His creation. The creation looks to Him, waits for Him, bows before Him, surrenders to His control, and simply does as He directs.

The oceans stay within the boundaries He has established for them. The grass and the trees grow according to God's direction and provide nourishment for man and animals, also in surrender to God's will. The sun and moon keep their appointed seasons; the animals get up when God tells them to get up and they lie down when God directs them to do so.

What is the result? "The earth is satisfied" (v. 13); "they are filled with good" (v. 28). Did you catch that? To surrender to the Creator's control is not onerous or burdensome; it is, in fact, the place of blessing, fullness, and peace. There is no evidence in this passage of any stress, struggle, or strain. Why? Because the creation is not vying with the Creator for control.

Don't miss this picture. It is what the old gospel song describes as "perfect submission, perfect delight!"[2]

THE BATTLE BEGINS

Let's go back to the Genesis account. The first blip on this perfect screen came when one of God's created beings—already a rebel himself—approached the happy couple and challenged God's created order. Until that point, there had never been any question about who was in charge and who was taking direction. Now the suggestion was made that the man and woman could be in charge of their own lives, that they didn't have to take direction from anyone else. *You don't have to live a surrendered life; you can be in control,* the tempter implied.

So the man and the woman—created beings—tried to wrest control from the hands of their sovereign Creator. Control that didn't belong to them. They resisted the will of God and insisted on sharing His throne. The battle had begun.

From that point to this, man has been engaged with his Creator in a battle for control—dueling wills, we might call it.

Mercifully, we are dealing with a Creator who is not only sovereign, but also compassionate. God knew that if we tried to run our own lives, we would reap misery and conflict, and that our drive to be in control would render us hopelessly enslaved and would ultimately destroy us. He knew that the only hope for man was through surrender.

From that very first skirmish, God set into motion a plan devised in eternity past to restore man back to a place of surrender to His control. Possessing absolute power, He could have chosen to bludgeon His rebellious creatures into submission. However, because He desires a loving, personal relationship with men and women, created in His likeness, He has opted first to woo and win the hearts of His creatures. He wants their willing, volitional surrender.

> GOD HAS OPTED FIRST TO WOO AND WIN THE HEARTS OF HIS CREATURES.

We know that one day "every knee [will] bow" and "every tongue . . . confess that Jesus Christ is Lord" (Philippians 2:10–11). Those who refuse His overtures of love and grace will do so under coercion. But those who love and trust Him will find ultimate, eternal joy in that glad-hearted surrender.

THE KING AND HIS KINGDOM

The very thought of God being bent on exercising control over His creation raises an obvious question. If you or I were to attempt to bring the whole planet under our control, we would rightly be labeled "control freaks." So why is it acceptable for God to insist on "world domination"? Why is it considered selfish and rebellious for us to want control, but absolutely appropriate for God to assert control? The answer is simple:

He's God—
and we're not.

In that profound, unalterable, eternal reality lies the key to understanding and dealing with this cosmic war, as well as handling our personal, daily struggles for control.

> HE IS THE ONLY ONE CAPABLE OF RUNNING THE UNIVERSE.

No one would consider it unreasonable for a mother to insist on being in control of her minivan while her four children are seat-belted in place. That's because she knows what she's doing. She knows how to drive and her children don't. She is the only one in the vehicle capable of keeping everyone safe. The fact that she doesn't share the driving with her preschoolers doesn't make her a control freak!

In the same way, God exercises His sovereign control over the universe because He is the only One capable of running the universe.

Inherent in His being is absolute sovereignty— the right to rule. He is the Creator—we are His creatures. He is eternal—we are finite. He is all-powerful

—we have no power of our own. He is autonomous, independent, and self-existent, needing no one and nothing—we are dependent on Him for our next breath (Acts 17:24–25).

The God revealed in the Scripture is King—not a king on a level with other kings, each with their own sphere of control—but *the* King over all kings. This King has a kingdom. That kingdom—the realm over which He has lawful jurisdiction—includes every molecule of the planet on which we live; it includes the farthest-flung reaches of our galaxy and of every galaxy; it includes those regions that are inhabited by the angelic hosts (both fallen and holy).

In his commentary on the Gospel of Luke, twentieth-century Bible expositor G. Campbell Morgan suggests that the kingdom of God really means the *kingship of God.*

> It means that God is King now, and always. The Kingdom of God is in existence. God has never been dethroned; and this is what Jesus preached. . . . He was proclaiming the Kingship of God, the rule of God, the fact that the Lord reigneth. . . .
>
> What this age needs is the proclamation of the sovereignty of God, the Kingship of God, the Kingdom of God. . . . When a man yields himself up to that sovereignty, nobody can tyrannize over him.[3]

The concept of a Sovereign King who exercises absolute control over His subjects is one that our egalitarian, Western minds find difficult to embrace. We want to have a say in the matter—to vote for the leader of our choice. We don't want to bow before an all-powerful monarch. To the contrary, what we really want is to *be* the king—or at least to have a representative form of government.

But whether we buy into it or not, the sovereign rule of God and the lordship of Jesus Christ is a nonnegotiable reality that is as determinative and binding as the law of gravity—and more so. It is an irrefutable truth with which every human being must come to terms, sooner or later. And, as Morgan suggests, those who resist His sovereign Lordship set themselves up to be tyrannized by other lords.

One Woman's Control Crisis

"Lynda," a forty-something mother of four, learned the hard way that to resist surrender to the perfect will of God is to become controlled by tyrants. I received a letter from Lynda in which she told her story. She has been married for twenty-five years to a man she calls "saintly." However, she grew up in a home with an alcoholic father who extremely controlling of her and her passive mother.

As she became an adult, she resolved that she

would never submit to another human. She recalls, "I had a huge problem when it came time to say our wedding vows—'to love and obey.' Love? Yes, absolutely! *Obey?* I don't think so!"

In retrospect, Lynda can see how her drive to be in control created numerous problems from the outset of her marriage and led to choices that ultimately caused her life to career out of control. She admits that she began to turn to other men

> to make me feel in control again, and to show my husband that I—and no one else—was in charge of my life. Little did I realize that I was "out of control" in many ways—including sexually and with alcohol abuse. And I was not ever in charge of my life or body.
>
> You see, while I refused to submit to my husband, I *was* submitting to other men—but not in loving relationships. I was not in control of my body or my life—other men were. "Meet me here, Lynda." "OK." "You drive today, Lynda." "OK." "You check us in at the motel." "OK." "Wear this, do that, call me. . . ." "OK, OK, OK."

Lynda's experience poignantly illustrates that as long as we refuse to surrender our will to the will of God, we are never truly free. Rather, we find ourselves dominated by ungodly appetites and forces.

When we throw off the restraints of our wise, loving God, we become slaves to terrible taskmasters that are intent on our destruction. That is exactly what happened to the Old Testament Israelites:

> *Because you did not serve the LORD your God joyfully and gladly in the time of prosperity, therefore in hunger and thirst, in nakedness and dire poverty, you will serve the enemies the LORD sends against you. He will put an iron yoke on your neck until he has destroyed you.*
>
> —Deuteronomy 28:47–48 NIV

You don't want to surrender to God's control? You won't bow to His will in relation to your marriage, your morals, your attitudes, your tongue, your eating habits, your spending habits, or the way you spend your time? Then count on it—the very points on which you refuse to surrender will become "enemies" that rule over you—lust, greed, possessions, food, sloth, immorality, anger, etc.

After more than twenty years of turmoil in every area of Lynda's life, the Lord brought matters to a head by causing her husband to discover her unfaithfulness. In an incredible display of the heart and ways of God, her husband not only extended mercy, but he tenderly and firmly exerted the wise, loving leadership that Lynda needed to get her life back in order.

Lynda hardly knew how to respond to such grace. But in that crisis of surrender, she says, "I repented. I knew I had to submit completely to God and to my husband—in that order!"

WHAT IS THE TURF IN WHICH YOU ARE IN A BATTLE FOR CONTROL?

Though she had always feared what would happen if she were to relinquish control of her life, Lynda began to experience blessings she had never known in all the years she was trying to hold on to the reins.

> A *huge* weight was lifted off my shoulders. I didn't want to be in control any more. My journey has not always been easy, but it has been wonderful and life-changing. I had to "let go" of a lot of people in my life—but I have God and my family. I have a beautiful peace of mind and serenity. And I hold my head high every day, because I know I have been forgiven. I will *never* be the same person again—ever.

Lynda's whole perspective on this matter of control has changed. Today she tells others, "Even if you are stubborn and think you will not submit to anyone, you will always be submitting to someone or something—and that can be extremely dangerous. Even life-threatening."

Surrendering her will to Christ's control in relation to her marriage brought about a dramatic change in Lynda's life. "Your kingdom come; Your will be done" replaced her former motto of "I am in charge of my own life."

What is the turf in which you are in a battle for control? Perhaps it is in relation to your marriage—you may be bent on changing your mate, refusing to accept him/her as God's choice for your life, or resisting your God-given responsibilities in that relationship.

Your battle for control may be in another relationship—perhaps with a parent, a child, an employer, a pastor, or a friend.

Or you may be resisting God's right to control your body—your eating, sleeping, exercise, or moral habits—or your tongue, your time, your future plans, or your finances.

Whether in our relationships, personal disciplines, daily decisions, or recurring habit patterns, our choice to resist or to voluntarily surrender to the control of the King has far-reaching implications.

When we play "king"—when we insist on establishing our own kingdom and asserting our right to rule—we set ourselves unavoidably at war with the Sovereign God of the universe—a battle, I might add, that we cannot possibly win. Invariably, we will end up being ruled by tyrants.

However, when we bow to His kingship—when we recognize His kingdom as being supreme, when we surrender to His wise and loving control—then we can live at peace with the King. And only then will we be free from all other tyrannies.

MAKING IT PERSONAL . . .

❋ What is one example of a battle for control in your life?

❋ What is one area of your life that has ended up ruling you as a "tyrant" because of your lack of surrender?

NOTES

1. Oswald Chambers, *My Utmost for His Highest,* September 13.
2. Fanny J. Crosby, "Blessed Assurance."
3. G. Campbell Morgan, *The God Who Cares* (Old Tappan, N.J.: Revell, 1987), 153, 172.

THE TERMS OF CHRISTIAN SURRENDER:
UNCONDITIONAL AND LIFETIME

I have been before God,
and have given myself,
all that I am and have,
to God; so that I am not,
in any respect, my own. . . .
I have given myself clear away,
and have not retained
any thing as my own.

*

JONATHAN EDWARDS[1]

*

The home of Wilmer and Virginia McLean in the village of Appomattox Court House, Virginia, was the scene of a historic meeting that resulted in bringing to an end the bloodiest conflict in this nation's history. On April 9, 1865, after four years of hostilities that had claimed some 630,000 lives and inflicted more than one million casualties, General Robert E. Lee signed an agreement surrendering the Confederate Army of Northern Virginia to General Ulysses S. Grant.

That defining moment in the Civil War was the culmination of an intense series of exchanges between the two commanders. Six days earlier, Richmond had fallen to Union troops. The battle continued as Lee led his army in retreat, pursued by

Grant and his men. On April 7, Grant sent a message to Lee suggesting that further resistance by the Confederate Army was hopeless and requesting that Lee surrender his portion of the army, to avoid further bloodshed.

Although Lee would not concede that his situation was hopeless, he responded the same day by asking Grant to spell out the conditions of any possible surrender.

In his reply early the following morning, Grant clearly stated the terms for surrender:

> Peace being my great desire, there is but one condition I would insist upon—namely, that the men and officers surrendered shall be disqualified for taking up arms against the Government of the United States.

Grant offered to meet Lee at any place he wished, for the purpose of working out the details of the surrender.

Lee responded later that day by saying that he wished to meet Grant at 10 o'clock the following morning to discuss how to bring about the "restoration of peace," but that he did not intend to surrender.

Grant's response early the next morning, April 9, made it clear that there was no point in meeting if

Lee was not willing to surrender. Grant appealed to the Southern commander to accept his conditions:

> The terms upon which peace can be had are well understood. By the South laying down their arms, they would hasten that most desirable event, save thousands of human lives, and hundreds of millions of property not yet destroyed.

Within hours, a messenger overtook Grant on the road to Appomattox Court House with Lee's reply. The inescapable reality was that Lee's army was surrounded and his men were weak and exhausted. His army was badly in need of food and basic provisions for both men and animals. Lee was left with little choice but to agree to meet for the purpose of surrendering.

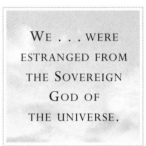

WE . . . WERE ESTRANGED FROM THE SOVEREIGN GOD OF THE UNIVERSE.

Lee's decision to accept Grant's terms of surrender that afternoon resulted in the conclusion of the Civil War, as Lee's Army of Northern Virginia laid down their arms, followed over the next few months by the surrender of the remaining Confederate armies.

Of course, an arduous, lengthy process of rebuilding the divided Union lay ahead. Nonetheless, at that decisive moment, once the terms of surrender were accepted, the course of the war and of the Union was changed and the ultimate outcome was assured.

PEACE THROUGH SURRENDER

Lee's surrender paved the way for peace to be restored to a war-torn nation. In the spiritual realm, there can be no peace with God, nor can there be peace in our hearts, apart from unconditional surrender. Refusing to surrender merely compounds our losses; delayed surrender only prolongs the conflict.

According to the Scripture, from the moment we were conceived, we were at war with God (Psalm 51:5). We had conflicting goals, desires, philosophies, strategies, and loyalties. Our will was opposed to His will. We were intent on going our own independent way, and as a result, were estranged from the Sovereign God of the universe.

Even when the Spirit opened our eyes to recognize our rebellious condition, we may have sought a way to bring about peace apart from surrender. We did not want to continue suffering the unpleasant consequences of our resistance, but neither did we want to lay down our arms.

Then the message was sent to our hearts: *There can be no peace until you are willing to accept My terms—unconditional surrender.*

Realizing that surrender was our best—and ultimately our only—option, we finally agreed to accept His terms. We waved the white flag; we owned Christ as Lord; we gave our lives to the One who gave His life for us on the cross—the One who demands and deserves our whole-hearted allegiance.

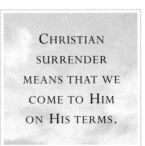

CHRISTIAN SURRENDER MEANS THAT WE COME TO HIM ON HIS TERMS.

The handover of power was not merely an external act, as was the case at Appomattox. Through an internal work of the Spirit and the grace of God, our willful, rebellious hearts were conquered and we were each given a new heart—a heart to love God and to obey and follow Christ as our Captain and sovereign Lord.

This is what the Bible calls being *born again—regenerated.* It is what theologians refer to as *conversion,* or what many people call the *point of salvation.* At that decisive moment, though he may not fully comprehend all that is taking place, the rebel repents of his anarchy against the King; the sinner surrenders to the loving lordship of his sovereign Creator and Savior.

In no way does that act of surrender save us. It is Christ's work on the cross, His sacrifice for sin, that is our only means of forgiveness and salvation. But His death is the provision that frees us from sin and enables us—yes, compels us—to surrender ourselves wholly to God.

The person who has never acknowledged Christ's right to rule over his life has no basis for assurance of salvation. He may claim to be a Christian; he may have walked an aisle or prayed the sinner's prayer; he may know how to speak "Christianese"; he may be heavily involved in Christian activities; but if he thinks he can have a relationship with God by retaining control over his life and somehow trying to fit Jesus in with everything else, he is deceived and is still at war with God.

Sadly, for the past 150 years or more, evangelicalism has developed a theology that offers assurance of salvation to almost anyone who prays a prayer or "makes a decision for Christ," even though he may still be clinging to his rights, holding on to his sin, and bent on running his own life. The Scripture does not recognize such a profession as genuine.

Jesus warned, "Not everyone who says to me, 'Lord, Lord,' will enter the kingdom of heaven, but only he who *does the will of my Father* who is in heaven" (Matthew 7:21 NIV, italics added). Surrender to the will of God is a mark of the truly converted.

The terms of our surrender to the Lord Jesus are nonnegotiable and unconditional. What does He ask us to surrender? In a word, *everything*. Christian surrender means that we come to Him on His terms, as the conquering general of our soul, and say simply, "I surrender all." We lay down our arms; we hand over everything we have, everything we are, everything we hope to be.

And, unlike Lee's surrender at Appomattox, our surrender to Christ does not involve a sense of genuine loss. To the contrary, Christian surrender brings us what we now see is beauty, life, joy, and true good. We are given eyes to see the glory of Christ we previously despised (2 Corinthians 4:4–6), and in surrendering to Him, we finally see the "surpassing value" of Christ over all that the world ever could have given us (Philippians 3:8 NASB).

FOUNDATION FOR A LIFETIME OF SURRENDER

As every believer soon discovers, that initial point of surrender to the Lord Jesus is not the final chapter—any more than Robert E. Lee's signature on a piece of paper on April 9, 1865, immediately resolved all the deep issues between the Union and the Confederacy.

As we have indicated, that crucial point must be followed by an ongoing process of working out the reality of our surrender in practical, day-to-day ways. However, that daily lifestyle of surrender is birthed out of a foundational, unconditional, lifetime surrender to Jesus as Lord.

I have seen this to be true in my own life.

My first conscious memory is kneeling by my bed on May 14, 1963, as a four-year-old child, and trusting Christ as my Savior. I don't recall the words I prayed that day—I'm sure they didn't reflect any deep theological understanding. But I had been nurtured in an environment of the Word of God, which the Spirit of God had used to show me my sinful condition and to draw my heart to Christ, who was my only hope.

Throughout those early years following my conversion, I had a growing, inescapable awareness that my life belonged to God, and by the age of seven or eight, I was conscious of having made a volitional, lifetime, unconditional surrender to Jesus as Lord of my life. That surrender was the fruit of the seeds of repentance and faith that God had planted in my heart when I was born again.

At that young age, I had little comprehension of the implications of full surrender. I had no idea what God would ask of me down the road. What I did know was that Jesus is Lord, that my life belonged to Him, and that to surrender myself completely to One who possessed infinite wisdom, love, and power was the only course that made any sense. With all my heart, I knew that I wanted to follow Christ—*whatever that might mean, whatever it might require, and wherever it might lead me.*

As my faith has matured, I have faced many

situations that have required a fresh affirmation and expression of that initial surrender to the will of God. Most of those instances have been simply the daily choices to obey the Word of God and the promptings of His Spirit. . . .

* Hold your tongue—don't try to prove your point.

* You've had enough to eat—stop!

* Assume the best of that person—don't give a negative report.

* Open your home to that couple who need a place to stay.

* Spend time in the Word and prayer before starting the business of your day.

* Seek forgiveness from that person you treated roughly.

* Make a financial contribution to that young person going on a mission trip.

On occasion, the pathway of obedience has required a more costly surrender.

* Forgive that person who defamed your reputation.

❉ Go to that person who has a grievance against you and seek to be reconciled.

❉ Give a large portion of your personal library to a Third World pastor who has few books.

❉ Sacrifice the security and blessings of a home to travel in full-time itinerant ministry.

❉ Yield the right to be married and to have children of your own.

Whether large or small, those points of surrender over some forty years have been greatly simplified because of that initial surrender to the lordship of Christ when I was a little girl.

In the natural realm, the dieter who has made a firm commitment not to eat desserts has an easier time saying, "No, thank you!" when the tantalizing dessert tray is passed than the person who is frustrated with being overweight but has not determined his course of action.

In much the same way, once that lifetime surrender has been made, many of our battles will be much less difficult to fight, because the outcome—*Jesus is Lord*—has already been established. That fundamental acknowledgment of His sovereign right to reign and rule over us will serve us well as our allegiance to the King is tested on a daily basis.

SIGNING OUR SURRENDER

One of the challenges of complete surrender to Christ is that we don't know what lies ahead. Doubtless, some of us might be more inclined to surrender if God would hand us a contract with all the details filled in. We'd like to know what to expect: "What will this cost me? Where will God expect me to go? What will He ask me to do?" We want to see all the fine print so we can read it over, think about it, and then decide whether to sign our name on the dotted line.

WE HAVE NOTHING TO LOSE BY SIGNING THE BLANK CONTRACT.

But that's not God's way. God says instead, "Here's a blank piece of paper. I want you to sign your name on the bottom line, hand it back to Me, and let Me fill in the details. Why? Because I am God; because I have bought you; because I am trustworthy; because you know how much I love you; because you live for My glory and not your own independent, self-promoting pleasure."

Signing that blank paper is risky . . . *if* God dies or *if* He ever falls off His throne or *if* He is not, in fact, trustworthy. But the reality is that we have nothing to lose by signing the blank contract. Oh, we may lose some things that the world considers valuable or essential. But in the eternal scheme of things, we cannot lose, because He is a God who can be completely trusted. If we will let Him, God will fill in the details of our lives with His incomparable wisdom and sovereign plan, written in the indelible ink of His covenant faithfulness and love.

THOSE WHO SIGNED THE CONTRACT

Some of the most stirring language in the pages of church history has come from the pens and hearts of men and women expressing their desire to be unreservedly surrendered to God.

For example, in 1753, John Wesley, greatly used of God in the first Great Awakening, published a "Covenant Prayer," based on a Puritan text written almost one hundred years earlier:

> I am no longer my own, but thine.
> Put me to what thou wilt, rank me with whom thou
>   wilt.
> Put me to doing, put me to suffering.
> Let me be employed by thee or laid aside for thee,
> Exalted for thee or brought low by thee.
> Let me be full, let me be empty.
> Let me have all things, let me have nothing.
> I freely and heartily yield all things to thy pleasure
>   and disposal.

And now, O glorious and blessed God,
Father, Son, and Holy Spirit,
Thou art mine, and I am thine. So be it.
And the covenant which I have made on earth,
Let it be ratified in heaven. Amen.[2]

French missionary Charles de Foucauld (1858–1916) expressed his heart this way:

Father, I abandon myself into Your hands; do with
me what You will. Whatever You may do, I thank
You: I am ready for all, I accept all. Only let Your
will be done in me, and in all Your creatures—I wish
no more than this, O Lord.

Betty Scott grew up in China, where her parents
were missionaries. She returned to the United States
at the age of seventeen for her last year of high school,
followed by college and Bible institute. During those
years, Betty penned a prayer that has become the petition of many other believers who long to live a life of
unconditional surrender to Jesus as Lord:

Lord, I give up my own plans and purposes, all my
own desires, hopes and ambitions, and I accept Thy
will for my life. I give up myself, my life, my all,
utterly to Thee, to be Thine forever. I hand over to
Thy keeping all of my friendships; all the people

whom I love are to take second place in my heart.
Fill me now and seal me with Thy Spirit. Work out
Thy whole will in my life at any cost, for to me to
live is Christ. Amen.

After completing her schooling, Betty returned to
China to serve with the China Inland Mission. Two
years later, in October of 1933, she married John
Stam, also a CIM worker. In December of 1934, just
weeks after the birth of their baby girl, John and
Betty were taken hostage by hostile Communist soldiers, and within a few days were beheaded. Betty
was twenty-eight years old.

When she wrote, "Work out Thy whole will in
my life *at any cost*," she had no way of knowing what
full surrender would cost her. Although some might
consider the cost exorbitant, I am confident that
Betty, having laid down her life for Christ, would not
think the price too high.

Fourteen years after the death of John and Betty
Stam, another young couple exchanged wedding
vows in a small town in Oklahoma. Although they
were deeply in love, at that point their focus was different from the Stams'. By his own admission, as a
young adult, Bill was motivated by selfish goals and

materialistic pursuits. When they got engaged, this enterprising young man had promised his wife-to-be that she would have everything her heart could desire—they would travel the world and own a home in upscale Bel Air, California.

However, during the first two years of their marriage, their desires and interests slowly began to change. Looking back nearly fifty years later, Bill explained what brought about the change: "We had both fallen in love with Jesus."[3]

At the time, Bill was pursuing a graduate degree at a nearby theological seminary, while also running a successful business he had started. Both he and his wife found themselves deeply stirred and motivated by the challenge of the Lord Jesus, recorded in the Gospel of Mark:

> *"If any of you wants to be my follower," he told them, "you must put aside your own pleasures and shoulder your cross, and follow me closely. If you insist on saving your life, you will lose it. Only those who throw away their lives for my sake and for the sake of the Good News will ever know what it means to really live."*
>
> Mark 8:34–35 TLB

One Sunday afternoon in the spring of 1951, as the young couple talked, they were gripped by the realization that knowing and serving the Lord Jesus was more important than any other pursuit in life. There in the living room of their home, they knelt together and prayed a simple, but heartfelt prayer:

> Lord, we surrender our lives irrevocably to You
>   and to do Your will.
> We want to love and serve You with all of our
>   hearts
> for the rest of our lives.[4]

At that moment, the kneeling pair could not have imagined the extent to which that prayer and the surrender it represented would change the whole course of their lives.

Bill describes one further step they took that day as an expression of their hearts' intent:

> We actually wrote and signed a contract committing our whole lives to Him, relinquishing all of our rights, all of our possessions, everything we would ever own, giving to Him, our dear Lord and Master, everything. In the words of the Apostle Paul, [my wife] and I became that Sunday afternoon voluntary slaves of Jesus.[5]

Once that contract was signed, the die was cast. There was to be no turning back. Decades later, Bill and Vonette Bright had become household names in the Christian world; they had founded and led one of the largest Christian organizations in history, with seventy different ministries, 26,000 full-time staff, and 226,000 trained volunteers serving in 190 countries of the world. Yet, in spite of his many achievements, when Dr. Bright was diagnosed with a terminal lung disease, he made it known that the only epitaph he and his wife wanted on their tombstone was "Slaves of Jesus Christ."

Bill and Vonette Bright have never served Christ out of a sense of drudgery or mere duty. Passionate love for Christ has been the spring of their desire to be His devoted slaves. In our day of Christian celebrities, public relations campaigns, and nationally telecast awards ceremonies, few professing believers are enthralled with the idea of being simply a slave of Jesus Christ. However, as we will see, if we overlook or reject that calling, we forfeit one of life's greatest privileges and our only means to true freedom.

MAKING IT PERSONAL . . .

* In your own words, write out a prayer expressing your heart's intent to be wholly surrendered to Christ. Then date and sign your "contract" with the Lord.

Notes

1. *The Works of Jonathan Edwards, Volume 1,* "Memoirs of Jonathan Edwards: Chapter IV: His Diary" (Carlisle, Pa.: Banner of Truth Trust, 1976), xxv.
2. *The United Methodist Hymnal,* #607, taken from the Wesleyan Covenant Renewal Service; published in 1753 by John Wesley.
3. From an acceptance speech by Dr. William R. Bright, receiving the 1996 Templeton Prize for Progress in Religion. Delivered in Rome, Italy, at The Church of St. Maria in Trastevere, 9 May 1996.
4. Ibid.
5. Ibid.

A HOLE
IN THE EAR:
BONDSLAVES FOREVER

Lord, send me anywhere,
only go with me;
lay any burden on me,
only sustain me;
and sever every tie,
but the tie that binds me
to Thy service and Thy heart.

❊

DAVID LIVINGSTONE

❊

Romanian pastor and Christian leader Josef Tson was exiled from his native country in 1981, after experiencing prolonged persecution at the hands of one of the most repressive Communist regimes in history. He immigrated to the United States, where he ministered for nearly a decade, until he was able to return to his homeland, where he continues serving today.

I first met Josef and his wife, Elizabeth, in the early 1980s when he was speaking to a gathering of Christian workers. I have never forgotten his response when he was asked how he wished to be introduced. Though his academic and professional credentials are impressive, Josef did not offer a printed bio sketch. Rather, this articulate, Oxford-educated theologian, who had suffered so greatly for his faith, said simply, "I wish to be introduced as 'a slave of Jesus Christ.'"

During his years in exile, Josef was taken aback by some of the traits of evangelical Christianity in the United States that were foreign to what he had experienced in Eastern Europe. As he studied the historical development of American evangelicalism, he discovered that those contemporary characteristics were the fruit of a series of spiritual paradigm shifts.

> THE EMPHASIS ON PURSUING HOLINESS SHIFTED TO A DESIRE FOR UPLIFTING, ECSTATIC EXPERIENCES.

The first of those changes took place at the beginning of the twentieth century, when the nineteenth-century emphasis on pursuing holiness shifted to a desire for uplifting, ecstatic experiences.

A second change took place in the 1950s and 1960s, which Josef identifies as a "shift from the call to *full surrender,* to the call to *commitment.*" He explains the difference this way:

> Christian *surrender* means that a person lifts his or her hands and says to God, "Here I am; I surrender; You take over; I belong to You; You dispose of me!"
>
> But this is America, the country of the independent people! This is the place of "Nobody should

command me! . . . I belong only to myself!"

A call to surrender, and even more, to full surrender, simply doesn't go well with such people.
Therefore, the preachers, who wanted "results," and
wanted them in big numbers, felt (and gave in to)
the temptation to soften the demand, to reduce the
cost, to make the message more "palatable." And
they hit the word "commitment."

You see, *commitment* means "I engage myself to
do something for you," or, even lighter, "I promise to
do something for you," but I remain myself and I
may keep my promise or not. We can speak of
weaker or stronger commitment, but be it as strong
as possible, it is still my independent self that
engages itself in a tentative promise.[1]

This subtle change paved the way for other shifts
in the Christian culture. Josef Tson goes on to say:

One of them came quietly, almost unobserved,
through the new versions of the Bible. Translators
did not like the term "bondslave" to be applied to
people. Who wants to be somebody else's slave?
Therefore, they replaced it with "servant." Again, a
reflection and demand of the independent spirit!

In the Greek, "slave" is *doulos;* "servant" is *diakonos.*
In the Greek Bible one never, never *diakoneo* to

God—one never *serves* God; one only *douleo* to God—that is, one *slaves* to God.

Jesus makes it clear in Luke 17 that however much you do for God, at the end of the day you say: "I am an unworthy slave; I only did what is the duty of the slave to do!" But all that is gone now, by the replacement of the word "slave" with the word "servant."

Webster's dictionary bears out the difference in meaning between these two words. A *servant* is defined as "a person employed to perform services . . . for another." A *slave,* on the other hand, is a "human being who is owned as property by and is absolutely subject to the will of another."

As Josef Tson points out, slavery is a concept we resist in the West. We can barely swallow the idea of a servant, but the word *slave* sticks in our throat— as it should, if we were speaking of coerced or involuntary slavery of a person who is owned against his will by another. That is an abhorrent relationship between two individuals, both of whom are created in the image of God. But it is absolutely appropriate that human beings should choose to be the slaves of the Lord Jesus, whom they love and long to serve for all their lives.

Pierced Ears

The twenty-first chapter of Exodus includes a lengthy list of regulations regarding Hebrew servants. Among them is a dramatic scenario that vividly illustrates what it means to be a bondslave in the spiritual sense:

> *Now these are the rules that you shall set before them. When you buy a Hebrew slave, he shall serve six years, and in the seventh he shall go out free, for nothing. . . . But if the slave plainly says, "I love my master, my wife, and my children; I will not go out free," then his master shall bring him to God, and he shall bring him to the door or the doorpost. And his master shall bore his ear through with an awl, and he shall be his slave forever.*
> —Exodus 21:1–2, 5–6 ESV

On occasion, poverty-stricken Jews were forced to sell themselves into service to their fellow Jews. The law of God required that all servants be treated with justice and kindness, and that they be freed at the end of six years. In this passage, we have a description of an unusual option provided for a servant who had fulfilled his obligation to his master and was due to be released from servitude.

The servant was free to leave. In this case, however, he had developed a strong, loving relationship with his master and with the wife and children he had acquired during his years of service, and he did not wish to be released from his master's service. Presumably, he admired his master and was grateful for the way he had been treated and provided for— so much so, that he wanted to continue serving in his master's household.

Knowing his master as he did, the bondslave trusted that all he needed would be provided, that he would never want for food, shelter, clothing, or any other basic needs.

> CHRIST HUM-
> BLED HIMSELF
> AND OFFERED
> HIMSELF TO BE
> A BONDSLAVE.

He was under no obligation to stay, but he *wanted* to stay—he *loved* his master and made a voluntary choice to become his master's *bondslave*. In doing so, he was not just signing up for another six-year stint— he was making a lifetime commitment. He was surrendering himself and giving up all his rights— permanently—to his master.

This was not merely a contractual agreement. This was not about being hired help. This was the act of a man who voluntarily said to someone he had come to know and love and trust, "I am yours—I belong to you, and I want to spend the rest of my life fulfilling your wishes."

There could be no secret about the nature of the

servant's new relationship to his master. The transaction was made in a public ceremony where the surrender was recognized in a visible—and painful —way. A sharp instrument was used to pierce a hole in the servant's ear, signifying obedience to the voice of his master. The decision was irreversible. From that point on, he would always be branded as a bondslave.

If the bondservant ever had second thoughts—if a week or a month, or a year, or ten years later he decided, "I think I want out of this deal"—he would always have a hole in his ear to remind him that he was not his own and never would be again. To acquire this mark of ownership involved a degree of suffering, but the servant was willing to endure the physical pain, in order to formally establish and demonstrate his relationship with his master. The hole spoke of lifetime ownership.

THE PICTURE FULFILLED

Nowhere in the Scripture or in ancient historical records do we find a single instance in which a servant made this choice referred to in Exodus 21. So why did God even suggest such a scenario? Like so many other Old Testament pictures, I believe it was intended to point us to Christ and to depict our relationship with Him.

The New Testament tells us that when the Lord Jesus came to this earth, He took "the form of a servant [*doulos*—the lowest form of slave]" (Philippians 2:7). In obedience to His Father's will and out of love for His Father—and for the bride and family His Father had given Him—He humbled Himself and offered Himself to be a bondslave, so He could deliver those who were in bondage to sin (Hebrews 2:10–18).

Speaking prophetically of the atoning death of Christ, the psalmist wrote, "Sacrifice and offering you did not desire, but *my ears you have pierced.* . . . I desire to do your will, O my God" (Psalm 40:6, 8 NIV, italics added). As far as we know, no one had ever opted to have his ear pierced in the ceremony described in Exodus 21—until *Christ* came to earth! In His desire to do the will of God and His willingness to suffer and bear the marks of that submission, He became the bondslave who symbolically fulfilled the literal exchange described in the Old Testament law.

In the New Testament, the apostles Peter and Paul, along with James and Jude (both half brothers of the Lord Jesus) all followed in the steps of that Great Bondslave when each identified himself as a *doulos*—a bond servant, a slave of Jesus Christ. Paul said, "I bear in my body the marks of the Lord Jesus" (Galatians 6:17). What was he saying? "I'm a man with a hole in my ear. I am the bondslave of Jesus Christ."

Certainly these men understood that they were also sons of God and coheirs with Jesus Christ—but, like Josef Tson, they wanted to be known first and foremost as the slaves of the Lord Jesus Christ.

No Higher Calling

I have come to believe that there is no greater calling than to be marked as His slave—to choose to give my life in the service of the Master I have grown to know and love and trust. For many years, my prayer has been, "Oh, God, make me a woman with a hole in my ear; I want to be identified as a slave of Jesus Christ."

That is not to say that living as a bondslave of Jesus Christ has always been easy. Among other things, for me, that choice has meant:

❋ Spending the majority of my adult life on the road, living out of suitcases in temporary accommodations

❋ Seldom being able to put down roots; difficulty maintaining deep, long-term relationships

❋ Relinquishing any "right" to a private life; virtually always being on display and "on call" to minister to the needs of others

❋ Living with relentless deadlines; little "free time" for entertainment, recreation, or personal pleasures; working when others are relaxing or socializing; few days or nights "off"

❋ Forgoing the privilege of marriage and childbearing

❋ Carrying an ever-pressing burden for the condition of the church and the spiritual needs of others

Do I sound as if I am complaining? I'll confess that I've done more than my share of whining about the "pressures and demands" of serving Christ, but the foundational reality that both motivates and drives my choices is the same perspective that motivated that bondservant in Exodus 21: *I love my Master!* I truly cannot imagine a more wonderful, gracious, kind, giving, loving Lord than He.

Are His requirements sometimes hard? Absolutely. Are they sometimes different from what I would have chosen for myself? No question. Do I sometimes wish to be free from the constraints placed upon me in His service? Definitely. Yet, in the deepest part of my heart, I truly want nothing more than to be His lifelong, loyal bondslave.

Now don't think that makes me some kind of supersaint. Nothing He has ever required of me could begin to repay the debt I owe Him. Besides, the heart He has given me ought to be—and can be— the heart of every child of God.

And, by all means, don't feel sorry for me! I can hardly begin to calculate the incredible gifts and joys He has lavished upon me since I first became His willing slave as a young girl. What a privilege it is:

❊ To know and love Him, and to be known and loved by Him

❊ To have His companionship at all hours of the day and night

❊ To live under His watchful, protective care

❊ To bring Him pleasure

❊ To be entrusted with the infinite riches of His glorious gospel and to be called to make it known to others

❊ To have an eternal home awaiting me in heaven

❊ To serve alongside so many precious fellow servants

❊ To have assisted in the birth and nurture of countless spiritual children

These are just a handful of the treasures I have received from His hand. Would I not be a fool to leave His service and choose to serve anything or anyone else in this world? As C. S. Lewis reminds us,

> Those Divine demands which sound to our natural ears most like those of a despot and least like those of a lover, in fact marshall us where we should want to go if we knew what we wanted.[2]

For you to be the slave of Jesus Christ will likely mean a different set of assignments than those He has given me or someone else. We must resist the temptation to compare what He asks of us with what He may require of others. He may ask you, as His bond servant, to:

❊ Forgo a fulfilling career or to make a name for yourself, in order to devote the prime years of your life to serving your husband and children

❊ Be "on call" 24/7 to meet the needs of your children or an elderly parent, having "no life of your own"

❋ Get out of your comfort zone and teach a Sunday school class or lead a small-group Bible study or develop an outreach to inner-city "at risk" youth

❋ Serve Him in a secular work environment that is antagonistic to Christian beliefs and values, or to be a faithful witness as the only believer in your extended family

❋ Serve faithfully for years in a needed but thankless and obscure position in your local church

❋ Reduce your living expenses so you can give more generously to the Lord's work

Regardless of whether He calls you to serve Him in ways that seem menial or significant, hidden or visible, beneath your skills or light-years beyond your abilities, routine or exciting, common or unimaginable . . . whatever He asks, wherever He sends . . . the surrendered heart will say with Mary of Nazareth,

> *"I am the bondservant* [marginal note] *of the Lord;*
> *Let it be to me according to your word."*
>
> —Luke 1:38 ESV

Leonard Ravenhill was a faithful servant of the Lord whose books and sermons on revival have inflamed the hearts of millions. At four o'clock one morning, just days before he went to meet the Master at the age of eighty-nine, he penned these words that I have displayed in my study as a reminder of what it means to be a bond servant of the Lord:

> Lord, engage my heart today
> with a passion that will not pass away.
> Now torch it with Thy holy fire
> that nevermore shall earth's desire
> invade or quench the heaven born power.
> I would be trapped within Thy holy will,
> Thine every holy purpose to fulfill,
> that every effort of my life
> shall bring rapturous praise to my eternal King.
> I pledge from this day to the grave
> to be Thine own, unquestioning slave.

Lord, grant that this prayer shall be our own. Amen.

MAKING IT PERSONAL . . .

* Are you a man/woman with a "hole in your ear"?

* Would your relationship with Christ be better characterized by the word *commitment* or *surrender?*

NOTES

1. E-mail from Josef Tson, 30 July 2001. In his book *The Closing of the American Mind,* university professor Allan Bloom makes a similar point from a secular perspective: "Commitment is a word invented in our abstract modernity to signify the absence of any real motives in the soul for moral dedication. Commitment is gratuitous, motiveless, because the real passions are all low and selfish" (New York: Simon & Schuster, 1987), 122.
2. C. S. Lewis, *The Problem of Pain* (London & Glasgow: Collins Clear-Type Press, 1940), 41.

THE WHOLE
OF OUR LIVES:
A LIVING SACRIFICE

We must train men and women
who will devote to the revolution,
not merely their spare evenings,
but the whole of their lives.

In 1917, a small handful of men set out to bring about a worldwide revolution. Within just a few decades, they had succeeded in building an empire that held more than one-third of the world's population in its grip. How did it happen?

At least in part, the answer lies in their devotion to a cause and their willingness to sacrifice their lives for that cause. Their mission and the outcome of their efforts were undeniably evil. Yet the rise of the Communist Party is one of the most striking examples in human history of the meaning of total surrender.

Douglas Hyde was a one-time Communist Party leader in England. In 1947, he defected from the party and spent the rest of his life endeavoring to expose the movement. In his thought-provoking book, *Dedication and Leadership,* Hyde highlighted some of the principles practiced by the Communist Party that he felt Christians would do well to embrace.

The theme of wholehearted dedication and sacrifice is a recurring one in Hyde's book. He pointed out, for example, that "practically every party member is a dedicated man in whose life, from the time he rises in the morning until the time he goes to bed at night, for 365 days a year, Communism is the dominant force."[2] Hyde described Communists as "100 percenters in a world of 50 percenters."[3]

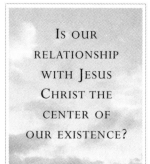

Is OUR RELATIONSHIP WITH JESUS CHRIST THE CENTER OF OUR EXISTENCE?

Years ago, I came across a letter written by a young Communist Party member to his fiancée, explaining why he felt compelled to break off their engagement. His letter illustrates the type of sacrificial mind-set that was characteristic of many who devoted themselves to the Communist revolution:

> There is one thing about which I am in dead earnest and that is the Socialist cause. It is my life, my business, my religion, my hobby, my sweetheart, my wife, my mistress, my bread and my meat. I work at it in the daytime, I dream of it at night. Its

hold on me grows, not lessens as time goes on. I shall be in it the rest of my life.

When you think of me, it is necessary to think of Socialism as well because I am inseparably bound to it. Therefore, I can't carry on a friendship, a love affair, or even a conversation without relating it to this force which both drives and guides my life. I evaluate people, books, ideas and notions according to how they affect the Socialist cause and by their attitude toward it.

I've already been in jail because of my ideas, and if necessary, I'm willing to go before a firing squad. A certain percentage of us get killed or imprisoned; even for those who escape these harsher ends, life is no bed of roses. A genuine radical lives in virtual poverty. He turns back to the party every penny he makes above what is absolutely necessary to keep him alive. Radicals don't have the time or money for many movies or concerts or t-bone steaks or decent homes or new cars.

We've been described as fanatics. We are. Our lives are dominated by one great over-shadowing factor—the struggle for Socialism.

The meteoric rise of Communism in our world cannot be explained, in my opinion, apart from a willingness to make what most would consider extreme sacrifices for a cause.

The example of those devoted to the cause of Communism prompts those of us who claim to believe the truth to examine our own level of sacrifice and surrender: Is our relationship with Jesus Christ the center of our existence? Like the young Communist, does our every act revolve around "the cause"— in our case, the cause of Christ?

SACRIFICES AND OFFERINGS

The Scriptures provide a number of word pictures that help us understand what it means to be a true follower of Jesus Christ. One of the most compelling images is that of a *burnt offering.*

Old Testament Jews knew all about sacrifices and offerings. Virtually every aspect of life—"secular" or "spiritual"—was tied in to a system of worship that revolved around sacrifices and offerings, words that appear in their various forms more than 1,600 times in the Old Testament alone.

Volumes have been written on the significance of the different offerings prescribed by God for His people. Ultimately, all those offerings were pictures intended to point people to their need for a Savior— an innocent One who would sacrifice His life as a substitute for sinners, making it possible for them to have fellowship with a holy God.

The most frequent form of sacrifice offered in the

Old Testament was the burnt offering (Leviticus 1), so-called because the sacrificial animal was placed on the altar and totally consumed by the fire.

Often offered in conjunction with sin or guilt offerings, burnt offerings were intended to express the worshiper's total dedication and consecration to the Lord. They pictured complete surrender to the will of God.

SACRIFICES PLEASING TO GOD

Though the New Testament does not speak explicitly of burnt offerings, it does reveal the fulfillment of that Old Testament picture in two senses. First, Christ, the Lamb of God, offered His body as a burnt offering, in complete consecration and surrender to the will of God (see Hebrews 9:14; 10:5–7). Second, in light of Christ's sacrifice for us, New Testament believers are exhorted to make an offering of their own:

> *Therefore, I urge you, brothers, in view of God's mercy, to offer your bodies as living sacrifices, holy and pleasing to God—this is your spiritual* [reasonable] *act of worship.*
>
> —Romans 12:1 NIV

This is the manifesto for the Christian's surrender to God. Our "bodies" represent the sum total of all that we are, all that we have, and all that we do. As those Old Testament believers signified their consecration by offering up sacrifices to be utterly consumed on the altar, so we are to offer ourselves in totality to be consumed by God.

Unlike the Old Testament sacrifices, however, we are to offer ourselves as *living sacrifices*—that is, we are to go on living in these bodies, recognizing that they are not our own, that they belong to God, whose temple we are.

This passage suggests both an initial and an ongoing aspect of consecration—a surrender that is made once and for all, as well as a daily, recurring sacrifice of our lives to God.

Offering our bodies speaks of a complete presentation of ourselves to God. It means devoting to the Lord Jesus, not just our "spare evenings," but "the whole of [our] lives."

Being a *living sacrifice* pictures living out that devotion, one day at a time, as God actually asks us for more than our "spare evenings," and we respond to Him on the basis of that initial consecration.

"I DO"—A MOMENT AND A LIFETIME

This twofold aspect of surrender—an initial point, followed by an ongoing, lifetime process—can be seen in marriage. When a man and woman stand before a minister to join their lives together, they affirm a series of vows, usually by saying "I do." At that moment, they make a full surrender of their lives to each other. They pledge to love each other, to be faithful to each other, and to serve each other.

The exchange of vows at the altar is just the starting place. But it *is* the starting place. Until a man and woman say "I do," they have no legal or spiritual basis for an ongoing, intimate, fruitful relationship.

WE ARE NEW PEOPLE, UNDER NEW OWNERSHIP, BOUND TO CHRIST ETERNALLY.

However, once a couple says "I do"—once they come to that point of initial surrender—they begin a lifetime process of keeping those vows, every day, for the rest of their lives. After the candles are blown out, the rice is thrown, and the rented tuxes are returned, they must begin to live out the implications of those vows in the nitty-gritty context of real life—for better *and* for worse.

Over time, they will grow in their understanding of what those vows really meant. Undoubtedly there will be moments when both partners will think back to the moment they stood at the altar and exchanged their vows, and will say to themselves, *I had no idea it would mean this! It never occurred to me that he would want me to do that! I never dreamed loving her would involve this!*

Likewise, in our relationship with the Lord, there is a starting place, a point at which we say to Him, "I do"; a point at which we enter into an eternal, covenantal relationship with Him. From that moment on, we are new people, under new ownership, bound to Christ eternally. Our lives are no longer our own; we belong to the One who created us and redeemed us by the blood of His Son.

Yet, at the point of conversion, no one can possibly be aware of all the implications of that transaction, any more than a couple standing at the altar is fully aware of all that their vows will mean down the road.

Our initial surrender to Christ was the launching pad for a lifetime of continual surrender and sacrifice. Now, on a daily, perpetual basis, we are called to live out that consecration, by responding to the various circumstances and choices of life in obedience and surrender to His will.

SACRIFICE—DIFFERENT SIZES AND SHAPES

One preacher illustrated the ongoing, daily dimension of sacrifice and surrender this way:

> We think giving our all to the Lord is like taking a $1,000 bill and laying it on the table—"Here's my life, Lord. I'm giving it all."
>
> But the reality for most of us is that he sends us

to the bank and has us cash in the $1,000 for quarters. We go through life putting out 25 cents here and 50 cents there. Listen to the neighbor kid's troubles instead of saying, "Get lost." Go to a committee meeting. Give up a cup of water to a shaky old man in a nursing home.

Usually giving our life to Christ isn't glorious. It's done in all those little acts of love, 25 cents at a time.[4]

God may be asking you simply to sacrifice the next thirty minutes to call your widowed mother-in-law who can be so negative . . . or your afternoon to help a family who is packing for a move . . . or your evening to help your child with a science project . . . or your normal night's sleep to care for a sick child . . . or your weekend to watch your neighbor's kids. . . . Twenty-five cents here. Fifty cents there.

At times, the Lord will ask you to lay down several quarters or even several dollars at once: Instead of taking that expensive vacation or buying that car or that new piece of furniture, give the money to a mission project or to a family in need . . . instead of settling into that comfortable retirement life, volunteer your services to a ministry in your local church or community . . . embrace God's gift of yet one more child . . . adapt your standard of living to make it possible for Mom to be at home with the children.

Periodically, the Lord may ask for a sacrifice that makes all the previous sacrifices seem insignificant: Quit your secure job and move your family to some place you never dreamed of living to serve the Lord in a mission organization . . . release your son or daughter to serve the Lord in a country where Christian witness is restricted . . . faithfully love your unbelieving mate who perpetually ridicules you and your faith . . . accept with gratitude the gift of a physically disabled child who will require constant, lifelong care . . . relinquish your dream of ever being able to conceive and bear children. . . .

Whether they fall in the category of twenty-five-cent pieces or hundred-dollar bills, the sacrifices God asks of us are never pointless. We can be assured that each one serves God's higher, eternal purposes for our lives and for the furthering of His kingdom. Realizing that every act of obedience is significant in God's economy and that it is all for *Him* will add a sense of purpose and joy as we bring our sacrifices and offerings.

A COMPLETE SACRIFICE

God's call to lay down our lives on the altar of sacrifice means that we give Him all that we are—our rights, our reputation, our desires, our future plans; everything that concerns us—first, for a lifetime, and then, day by day, moment by moment, decision by decision.

Dr. Helen Roseveare is one of my spiritual heroines. During the 1950s and 1960s, she served as a missionary doctor in Belgian Congo (now Democratic Republic of the Congo), where she suffered great atrocities during the Simba Rebellion. When I need to be reminded what it means to live a surrendered life, I go back and reread her compelling story, *Living Sacrifice*. Dr. Roseveare's practical description of what it means to be a living sacrifice applies to every believer—whether a missionary, a homemaker, a student, a business owner, or an office worker:

> To be a living sacrifice will involve all my time. God wants me to live every minute for Him in accordance with His will and purpose. . . . No time can be considered as my own, or as "off-duty" or "free." . . .
>
> To be a living sacrifice will involve all my possessions. . . . All should be available to God for the furtherance of His Kingdom. My money is His . . . He has the right to direct the spending of each penny. . . . I must consider that I own nothing. All is God's, and what I have, I have on trust from Him, to be used as He wishes.

To be a living sacrifice will involve all of myself. My will and my emotions, my health and vitality, my thinking and activities all are to be available to God, to be employed as He chooses, to reveal Himself to others. Should He see that someone would be helped to know Him through my being ill, I accept ill health and weakness. I have no right to demand what we call good health. . . . All rights are His—to direct my living so that He can most clearly reveal Himself through me. God has the right, then, to choose my job, and where I work, to choose my companions and my friends. . . .

> SHALL WE DEVOTE TO SUCH A SAVIOR ONLY OUR SPARE EVENINGS?

To be a living sacrifice will involve all my love. . . . I relinquish the right to choose whom I will love and how, giving the Lord the right to choose for me. . . . Whether I have a life partner or not is wholly His to decide, and I accept gladly His best will for my life. I must bring all the areas of my affections to the Lord for His control, for here, above all else, I need to sacrifice my right to choose for myself. . . .

I need to be so utterly God's that He can use me or hide me, as He chooses, as an arrow in His hand or in His quiver. I will ask no questions: I relinquish all rights to Him who desires my supreme good. He knows best.[5]

A Reasonable Response

Does that seem too much to ask? Truthfully, there are moments when I feel something God is asking of me is unreasonable. It may be to provide a listening ear and a caring heart for one more woman who wants to talk, when I am emotionally and physically spent at the end of a long day of ministry; it may be to provide substantial financial support to help a couple in Christian work provide a Christian education for their children; it may be to stay engaged in a relationship with a difficult, demanding person.

In those moments, my emotions sometimes cry out, "I've already given so much! I just can't give more." That's when I need to take a trip to Calvary and look into the eyes of a bleeding God who gave everything to reconcile me to Himself. That is why the apostle Paul says,

> *I urge you . . . in view of God's mercy, to offer your bodies as living sacrifices . . . this is your reasonable* [marginal rendering] *act of worship.*
>
> —Romans 12:1 NIV

The Greek word translated "reasonable" is the word *logikos.* In light of the incredible mercy of God poured out on us (past, present, and future mercies), a full and complete sacrifice of our lives is the only *logical* response we can make.

Willis Hotchkiss was a pioneer missionary in East Africa in the late 1800s who made what we would consider extraordinary sacrifices for the sake of Christ. On one occasion, he described some of the conditions he and others had faced in the early days of their work: living for more than two months on beans and sour milk, enduring without basic necessities for extended periods of time, fearing attacks from man-eating lions, watching many colleagues lose their lives. Then he concluded,

> But *don't talk to me about sacrifice.* It is no sacrifice. In the face of the superlative joy of that one over-whelming experience, the joy of flashing that miracle word, Saviour, for the first time to a great tribe that had never heard it before, I can never think of these forty years in terms of sacrifice. I saw Christ and His cross and I did this because I loved Him.[6]

God may never call you to a foreign mission field; He may never ask you to endure the conditions that Willis Hotchkiss faced in Africa. Nonetheless, He does ask that you offer up your life and your daily circumstances as a living sacrifice—a burnt offering —signifying your wholehearted consecration and surrender to the Savior who gave His life for you.

Shall we devote to such a Savior only our spare evenings? Is He not worthy of the whole of our lives? In the words of Isaac Watts's immortal hymn,

Were the whole realm of nature mine,
that were a present far too small.
Love so amazing, so divine,
demands my life, my soul, my all![7]

MAKING IT PERSONAL . . .

❄ Have you devoted to Christ "the whole of your life," or are you merely giving Him your "spare evenings"?

❄ What might it mean for you today to offer yourself as a "living sacrifice" to God?

NOTES

1. Cited in *The Whole of Their Lives,* epigraph. From *Lenin on Organization* (Daily Worker Publishing Co., 1926), 44. Lenin first wrote these words in the Social Democratic newspaper *Iskra,* No. 1, in 1900.
2. Douglas Hyde, *Dedication and Leadership* (Notre Dame, Ind.: Univ. of Notre Dame, 1966), 25.
3. Ibid., 40.
4. From a message at a Pastoral Leadership conference, given by Dr. Fred Craddock.
5. Helen Roseveare, *Living Sacrifice* (Minneapolis: Bethany, 1979), 116–18.

6. Cited in T. A. Hegre, *The Cross and Sanctification* (Minneapolis: Bethany, 1960), 179–80.

7. Isaac Watts, "When I Survey the Wondrous Cross."

FACING OUR FEARS:
FINDING HIM FAITHFUL

*If there is anything holding you
back, or any sacrifice you are
afraid of making, come to God and
prove how gracious your God is.
Never be afraid that
He will command from you
what He will not bestow!
God comes and offers to work
this absolute surrender in you.*

ANDREW MURRAY[1]

As I write this chapter, some of our Christian brothers and sisters in Indonesia are paying an enormous price to follow Christ. In certain villages that have been taken over by militant Muslims, Christians who refuse to convert to Islam are being "allowed" to leave their villages. The cost of that freedom is that they must forsake their homes and everything they own, and they may never again return to their villages. The only way they can stay is if they agree to become Muslims.

Such a price is unfathomable to most of us. We cannot conceive of being required to literally forsake everything for the sake of Christ. Nonetheless, when we consider Christ's call to full surrender, we may wrestle with real fears of what that might mean for us.

"I surrender all . . ."; "Christ is all I need. . . ." The words roll off our lips as we sing them in church. But it's not so easy to choose to place ourselves in a position where we have to find out if He really is all we need. Although we are not likely to find ourselves in the same situation as those Indonesian believers, full surrender to Christ forces us to face the possibility—or the reality—of giving up some of the things we consider most important in life.

Our natural tendency is to hold on tightly, to try to protect and preserve whatever we think we can't live without. We are afraid that if we surrender *everything* to God—our health, our material possessions, our family, our reputation, our career plans, all our rights, our future—He might take us up on it! We have visions of God stripping us of the things we most need or enjoy, or perhaps sending us out to serve Him in the most inhospitable place on the planet.

Many of our fears about relinquishing total control of our lives to God fall into four categories. If I surrender everything to Him, what about . . .

Provision—Will I have what I need? What if I lose my job? What if my husband loses his job? Can we afford to have more children? How will we pay for their education? What if God asks us to give our savings to the church or to a needy family? What if God calls us into vocational ministry—how will we be supported? What if the economy goes under—what will happen to our investments? What if my husband dies—will I have enough to live on?

Pleasure—Will I be happy? If I fully surrender to God, will I be miserable? Will I be able to do the things I enjoy? What if He wants me to give up my career . . . or sports . . . or my favorite hobby . . . or my best friend . . . or the foods I really like? Might God make me stay in this unhappy marriage? Will I be fulfilled if I obey Him?

Protection—Will I (and those I love) be safe? What if my child is born with a mental or physical disability? What if someone abuses my children? What if I have an accident and am maimed for life? What if I get cancer? What if someone breaks into our house? Might God choose to take my mate or my children? If my child goes to the mission field, will he be safe?

Personal relationships—Will my relational needs be met? What if the Lord wants me to be single all my life? How can I live without sex or romance? What if my mate never loves me? What if God doesn't give us children? What if I lose my mate? How can I handle the rejection of my parents? What if my best friend moves away? What if people reject our family because of our commitment to biblical standards?

Overcoming Fear with Faith

The pages of Scripture are salted with the stories of men and women who risked everything to follow Christ. Sometimes we think of these people as if they were merely lifeless figures in a wax museum; we forget that they were real people who had to deal with real-life issues.

Take Abraham, for example. We think of Abraham as a superhero—a man of towering faith. And he was. Yet he had to face many of the same issues and fears that we struggle with. Over and over again, in order to move forward in his relationship with God, Abraham was called to make a fresh surrender to God. To do so required that he let go, relinquish control, step out on a limb, and trust a God he could not see.

Abraham grew up in a pagan, idolatrous environment where there was absolutely nothing to inspire or nurture faith—no study Bibles, no praise and worship CDs, no churches, no Christian fellowship. When an unseen, unknown God spoke and told Abram (as he was known at the time) to venture out and leave behind everything that was familiar and comfortable, he was faced with a choice: to stay or to go.

In making that choice, Abram had to consider the cost of surrender:

❋ How will my family's needs be met?
   (*provision*)

❋ Will we be happy? (*pleasure*)

❋ Will we be safe? (*protection*)

❋ You want my wife and me to leave all our
   friends and relatives? (*personal relationships*)

The biblical record does not tell us to what
extent, if any, Abram wrestled with his decision. All
we know is that he went. Genesis 12:1 records God's
call to Abram: "Leave your country, your people and
your father's household" (NIV). Three verses later we
read, "So Abram left, as the LORD had told him"
(12:4 NIV).

Without further explanation, with no idea where
he was going, how he would get there, or what he
would do once he got there, Abram risked everything, cast himself into the arms of Providence . . .
and went. He chose friendship with God over all
human relationships, earthly attachments, and visible security.

"But," you say, "Abraham had a lot to gain—after
all, God had promised to give him a fruitful land
and more offspring than he could count." Yes,
Abraham was the recipient of grand promises. But
keep in mind that for more than twenty-five years,

he didn't have a shred of visible evidence that God's promises would be fulfilled. Acts 7:5 reminds us of the reality that could easily have shaken Abraham's faith: He had "no inheritance" and "no child." But he went anyway. And, in spite of occasional lapses in his faith, he kept going.

> THE PROMISES OF GOD PROVIDE A POWERFUL ANTIDOTE TO ALL OUR FEARS.

Abraham surrendered himself to the purposes and plans of God, with no tangible guarantee that his obedience would ever "pay off." Even when he could not see the outcome of his faith, he *believed God.* He staked his life, his security, his future—everything—on the fact that God was real and that He would keep His promises (Hebrews 11:6). That was the foundation on which his faith rested. That was what motivated his repeated acts of surrender.

It was faith in the character and the promises of God that enabled Abraham and his wife, Sarah, to embrace an itinerant lifestyle—living in tents—for more than twenty-five years.

It was faith in the promises of God that sustained the couple through decades of infertility and un-fulfilled longings.

It was faith in the promises of God that moti-vated Abram to surrender the best land option to his nephew Lot and to trust that God would provide a suitable inheritance for him (Genesis 13:1–11).

It was the character and the promises of God that gave Abram courage (at the age of seventy-five!) to take on the massive military machine of the allied kings of the East, in order to rescue his errant nephew (Genesis 14).

When Abram was tempted to fear reprisals from the defeated kings, God bolstered his faith with a rehearsal of His promises: "Do not be afraid, Abram. I am your shield, your exceedingly great reward" (Genesis 15:1). What was God saying? *I am your protection and your provision; if you have Me, you have all you need. So . . . trust Me!*

At times, the call of God in our lives may require us to relinquish things or people we can't imagine living without—material possessions, a job or a promotion, good health, a mate or a child, or the respect and understanding of our closest friends. The promises of God provide a powerful antidote to all our fears and free us to step out in faith and surrender.

STRANGER ON EARTH, FRIEND OF GOD

Abram came to be known by his contemporaries as "Abram the Hebrew" (Genesis 14:13). The word *Hebrew* means "stranger" or "alien." From earth's perspective, he was always something of a "misfit";

he didn't really belong. But that was OK. He understood that everything this world offers is temporary at best. His ultimate citizenship wasn't on this earth. He was living for an eternal home (Hebrews 11:16).

EACH "SMALL" STEP OF SURRENDER CONFIRMS THAT GOD IS WORTHY OF OUR TRUST.

He was willing to venture everything this world considers vital—homeland, reputation, position, possessions, family, prestige—in order to be eternally secure and to gain the blessing of God. And that is exactly what happened.

Though he was an alien on earth, from heaven's perspective Abraham was called the "friend of God" (James 2:23). The development of this man's extraordinary relationship with God can be defined in terms of a series of surrenders made over a lifetime. Each of those surrenders was based on a revelation of the promise-making, promise-keeping God.

ALTARS OF SURRENDER

Perhaps the most appropriate symbol of Abraham's life is an altar. On four distinct occasions, at different stages in his pilgrimage, we are told that Abraham responded to God by building an altar. First at Shechem (Genesis 12:7), then between Bethel and Ai (12:8), then at Hebron (13:18),

Abraham erected altars—silent symbols of surrender and faith.

Then, on a mountain named Moriah, the man who was called the "friend of God" built yet another altar (22:9). On that altar, at God's unmistakable, but incomprehensible direction, Abraham placed his own son. It was the ultimate act of surrender—a relinquishing of all he held dear.

In an act not unlike a resurrection, God spared Abraham's son. The test had been passed. God knew that when Abraham laid his precious, long-promised son on the altar and prepared to plunge the knife into his heart, Abraham himself was on the altar—all that he was and all that he had were God's.

All those earlier altars had been preparing Abraham for the moment when he would be called upon to make a supreme sacrifice. With each act of surrender, the trustworthiness of God and His promises had been established in Abraham's heart. Likewise, each "small" step of surrender that we take confirms that God is worthy of our trust and prepares us to trust Him with bigger surrenders that may be required down the road.

Altars speak of sacrifice and devotion—of being consumed. They speak of a life that is wholly given up to the one for whom the altar is built. Many churches identify a location or an object at the front of the sanctuary as an "altar." Though we don't light fires and offer literal sacrifices on those sites, they are intended to serve as visible reminders of what ought to be a spiritual reality for every child of God —as the hymn writer put it, "My heart an altar, and Thy love the flame."[2]

PROMISES THAT COUNTER OUR FEARS

The surrender points Abraham faced over the course of his life may be similar to some you have faced: leaving family and friends behind and moving to a new city where you didn't know a soul . . . making choices to sacrifice your own interests for the sake of others . . . staying engaged with and pursuing the heart of a rebellious relative . . . living with infertility . . . turning down a lucrative offer that you know is not pleasing to God . . . giving up the life of a child.

When it comes to the uncertainties that keep us from sacrifice, surrender, and slavery to God, we, like Abraham, have "exceedingly great and precious promises" (2 Peter 1:4) from God's Word—promises that powerfully counteract our deepest fears. If we trust those promises and the God who has made them, we will be given courage to make each sacrifice He asks of us.

If we do not trust God's promises and, therefore, do not step out in faith and surrender, we will ultimately find ourselves in bondage to the very things we refuse to surrender. We will end up being controlled by that which we are seeking to keep within our own control.

Trust or tyranny. That is the option. *Trust* the promises of God—which will free you to live joyfully under His loving lordship—or live under the *tyranny* of that which you will not surrender.

God wants us to experience provision, pleasure, protection, and personal relationships. But He wants us to seek them in the only place they can be found—in Him. And He doesn't want us to settle for substitutes for the real thing.

Provision. Scripture exhorts us to be content with what we have (Hebrews 13:5) and not to worry about how our future needs will be met (Matthew 6:25–34). The basis for contentment and freedom from anxiety is that God has promised to provide all that we need (though not necessarily all that we *want*) (Philippians 4:19). Based on His promise, when we have a need, rather than fretting, striving, or manipulating, we ought to simply and confidently ask Him to provide (Matthew 7:7; Philippians 4:6).

If we are unwilling to trust God in the matter of provision, we may be tyrannized by greed, stealing, cheating, lack of generosity, lying, worrying, coveting, or centering our lives around money.

Pleasure. We cannot escape the fact that pain is unavoidable in this fallen world and that suffering is an instrument that God uses to mold and sanctify those He loves. But God also created us to experience intense pleasure and joy. The problem is that we are prone to seek pleasure in things and people that cannot ultimately satisfy the deep longing in our hearts. For our hearts can never be truly satisfied with less than Him. The unsurrendered heart pursues after what are paltry pleasures, compared with the pure, infinite pleasures God wants to give us:

> THOSE WHO TAKE REFUGE IN HIM ARE PLACED UNDER HIS PROTECTION.

You will show me the path of life;
In Your presence is fullness of joy;
At Your right hand are pleasures forevermore.

How precious is Your lovingkindness, O God!
Therefore the children of men
    put their trust under the shadow of Your wings.
They are abundantly satisfied with the fullness of Your
    house,
And You give them drink from the river of Your pleasures.
                              —Psalms 16:11; 36:7–8

Even fully surrendered saints sometimes experience sorrow, suffering, and struggles. But in the midst of our earthly journey, the joy Christ offers lifts us beyond our circumstances and provides us with a breathtaking foretaste of heaven's eternal pleasures.

However, if we are unwilling to trust God with our happiness and well-being, and we insist on the pursuit of temporal pleasures, we may become dominated by overeating, getting drunk or using drugs, sexual promiscuity, adultery, pornography, obsession with television or films or novels, being irresponsible, or living beyond our means.

Protection. Our God is a refuge, a fortress, a shelter, and a strong deliverer to His children. Psalm 91 speaks of God's amazing protection:

> *I will say of the LORD, "He is my refuge and my fortress, my God, in whom I trust." . . . He will cover you with his feathers, and under his wings you will find refuge; his faithfulness will be your shield and rampart. You will not fear the terror of night, nor the arrow that flies by day, nor the pestilence that stalks in the darkness, nor the plague that destroys at midday.*
>
> —Psalm 91:2, 4–6 NIV

God doesn't promise that we will never face danger, but those who take refuge in Him are placed under His protection. He assures us that He will defend us and keep us free from fear, no matter what comes our way.

However, if we do not entrust our safety to God,

but demand human assurance of protection and security, we may be overwhelmed by fearfulness, worry, mistrust of people, obsession with weapons, unwillingness to be vulnerable, fear of intimacy, tendencies toward violence, hatred, prejudice, conspiracy theories, or paranoid-type thoughts.

Personal relationships. It is true that God may lead us into solitude for a season. But His Word makes it clear that an intimate relationship with Him is the basis for the richest of human relationships (1 John 1:3, 7). God Himself has promised to remain with us, to be our constant companion, wherever we go, whatever we do. "I will never leave you nor forsake you," He has vowed (Hebrews 13:5).

Throughout the Scripture, whenever one of His children was fearful to step out alone, without human support, God's simple response was, *I will be with you.* The implication was—*I am enough. If you have Me, you have everything you need.*

The man or woman who trusts His promises can say with the psalmist,

Whom have I in heaven but You?
And there is none upon earth that I desire besides You.
　　　　　　　　　　　　　　　　　—Psalm 73:25

If we do not value *Him* as our primary relationship, we will live in fear of losing human relationships and will set ourselves up to be tyrannized by such things as possessiveness, giving or taking abuse, adultery, promiscuity, gossip, obsessive or controlling relationships, lust, dissatisfaction, unforgiveness, bitterness, manipulation, dishonesty, or jealousy.

THINGS WE CAN COUNT ON

Ann Blocher was first diagnosed with breast cancer in 1977, when her five children were young adults. After going through chemotherapy, she went into apparent remission. Several years later, the cancer reappeared. After battling to control the cancer with chemo and diet, she finally went home to be with the Lord in 1986.

As she walked through those tempestuous and uncertain years, Ann had to face numerous fears about her future and her family. One of the things she struggled with was her desire to be a part of her children's lives. As she dealt with each issue, Ann discovered that the surrender God was asking of her really came down to a matter of trust. She expressed that perspective in a poem written less than three years before her homegoing:

Yes, Lord! Yes and Amen!

Can you trust Me, child?
Not only for ultimate eternity,

of which you know next to nothing,
and so are not tempted to meddle—
But for the little span of your life between
the Now and Then, where you envision
decline and separations and failures,
impairments, pain, bereavements, disappointments—
Do you find Me qualified to be Lord of your last days?
Oh—yes, Lord! YES, Lord! Yes and amen!

Can you trust Me, child?
Not only to synchronize the unthinkable
intricacies of creation—
But to work together for good the gravities
and tugs within your little orbit,
where your heart is pulled by needs
and lacks you wish, but are destitute, to fill—
Do you find My resources adequate
to feed both the sparrows and you?
Oh—yes, Lord! YES, Lord! Yes and amen!

Can you trust Me, child?
Not only for the oversight of nations
and creations not of this world—
But for those beloved ones I committed
to you and you committed to Me—
Do you believe Me trustworthy to perform
the good work begun in them
until the Day of Jesus Christ?
Oh—yes, Lord! YES, Lord! Yes and amen![3]

As Ann Blocher cast herself upon the character, the heart, and the promises of God, she was enabled to respond to the will of God in wholehearted surrender —whether that meant being sick or well, living or dying.

Isn't that the heart of the matter for every child of God? *Can you trust Me?*

Whatever your fears, whatever the unknowns or the challenges in your life, God has promised to provide for you, to share His pleasure with you, to protect you, and to give you His enduring presence.

The fact remains that when we sign the blank contract of surrender, there are no guarantees about where God will lead us or how difficult our journey will be. Yet we know the character of the One in whom we've placed our trust. And we know that God's promises more than offset any risks or dangers or challenges that He may allow into our lives.

MAKING IT PERSONAL . . .

❀ Which of the four fears identified in this chapter do you most relate to?

❀ How has that fear caused you to hold back from surrendering some part of your life to God?

❖ What is one promise in God's Word that addresses your fear?

NOTES

1. Andrew Murray, *The Believer's Absolute Surrender* (Minneapolis: Bethany, 1985), 78.
2. George Croly, "Spirit of God, Descend upon My Heart."
3. Permission for use granted by Betty and Clarence Blocher.

LIVING THE SURRENDERED LIFE:

MAKING IT PRACTICAL

Full consecration may be in one sense the act of a moment and in another the work of a lifetime. It must be complete to be real, and yet—if real— it is always incomplete.

Consecration is a point of rest and yet a perpetual progression.

FRANCES R. HAVERGAL[1]

One of the clearest statements of the practical terms of surrender for every follower of Christ is found in Luke 14. In verse 25, we find Jesus surrounded by a large crowd. Unlike what we might have been tempted to do, Jesus never played to the audience. He wasn't concerned about His ratings; He wasn't running for office or trying to attract the biggest crowd in town. He knew full well that when some heard His message, they would lose interest in His movement. But that didn't keep Him from being straightforward.

Jesus looked at the crowd of would-be disciples and said, in effect, "If you want to follow Me, you need to understand what's involved": "If anyone comes to me and does not hate his father and mother, his wife and children, his brothers and sisters"—and here's the heart of the matter—"yes, even his own life—he cannot be my disciple. And anyone who does not carry his cross and follow me cannot be my disciple" (vv. 26–27 NIV).

There could be no mistaking Jesus' point. He was not offering His listeners some sort of weekend Christian experience, an escape from their problems, an anesthetic for their pain, or fire insurance from hell. Everyone listening to Jesus knew that a cross meant only one thing—death. He was calling them to come and die to everything that competed with His reign and rule in their lives.

> IT IS IN THE LABORATORY OF LIFE THAT OUR INITIAL CONSECRATION TO CHRIST IS TESTED.

In verse 33 (NIV), He reiterated His call to total surrender: "Any of you who does not give up everything he has cannot be my disciple."

Jesus' words in Luke 14 are penetrating because they are so intensely personal and practical. He did not speak in sweeping generalities; rather, He identified specific issues that must be surrendered by those who call themselves His followers—things like our *relationships,* our *affections,* our *physical bodies,* our *rights,* and our *possessions.*

It's one thing to have an emotional experience at a Christian gathering where you are inspired and chal-

lenged to surrender control of everything to God. It's
another matter to live out that surrender once the
emotion of the moment has passed—when the bus
gets home from the conference . . . when you lose
your job and the bills keep coming . . . when you
find out you're expecting your fifth child in seven
years . . . when your mate is diagnosed with a terminal illness.

It is in the laboratory of life that our initial consecration to Christ is tested, proven, and demon-
strated in daily, moment-by-moment choices and
responses, as we surrender to the sovereignty and
will of God.

In 1874, when she was just thirty-eight years old,
Frances Ridley Havergal penned a hymn that has
become a beloved treasure of the church. Written as
a prayer, each line focuses on one dimension of what
it means to be fully surrendered to Christ. Like Jesus'
words in Luke 14, Frances Havergal's words answer
the question: *What does a surrendered life look like?*

The following questions are intended to help per-
sonalize and apply this wonderful text. I would
encourage you not to skim through these questions,
but to set aside some time for thoughtful, prayerful
reflection and response.

My Life

*Take my life, and let it be
consecrated, Lord, to Thee.*

❋ Have I ever consciously acknowledged
Christ's ownership of my life?

❋ Have I made a volitional, unconditional, lifetime surrender of my life to Christ?

❋ Am I seeking to live out that surrender on a
daily basis?

❋ Are there any "compartments" of my life over
which I am reserving the right to exercise
control?

My Time

*Take my moments and my days;
let them flow in ceaseless praise.*

❋ Do I live with the conscious realization that
all my time belongs to God, or have I merely
reserved a portion of my time for the "spiritual" category of my life?

❋ Am I living each day in the light of eternity?

❋ Am I purposeful and intentional in my use of time, seeking to invest the moments of my days in ways that will bring glory to God?

❋ Do I seek His direction as to how I should use my "free time"?

❋ Am I squandering time with meaningless, useless conversation or entertainment?

❋ Do I set apart time each day for worship, prayer, and personal devotion?

❋ Do I readily respond to opportunities to serve others, even if it requires sacrificing "my" time?

❋ Do I become resentful or impatient when others interrupt my schedule or when I am faced with unplanned demands on my time?

❋ Do I view my job as an opportunity to serve Christ and bring glory to God?

❋ Have I considered any possible vocational change the Lord may want me to make to devote more time to the advancement of His kingdom?

MY BODY

Take my hands, and let them move
at the impulse of Thy love.
Take my feet, and let them be
swift and beautiful for Thee.

❋ Am I yielding the members (parts) of my
body to God as instruments of righteousness
(Romans 6:13)?

❋ Do I use the members of my body to express
the kindness and love of Christ to others
(e.g., using my hands for serving, for gentle
touch)?

❋ Are any of the members of my body—eyes,
ears, hands, feet, mouth, etc.—being used to
sin against God (e.g., stealing, lying, listening
to or repeating gossip, inflicting physical
harm on mate or children, listening to pro-
fanity, viewing pornography, sexual sin)?

❋ Do I treat my body as if it is the temple of
the Holy Spirit (1 Corinthians 6:19)?

❋ Am I abusing my body in any way (e.g., with
food, alcohol, illegal or prescription drugs)?

❋ Am I willing to be physically spent in serving
God and others?

✷ Have I relinquished the right to have a healthy body? Would I accept and embrace physical illness if that would bring glory to God?

✷ Am I submissive to God in relation to what (and how much) I eat and drink, and how much and when I sleep?

✷ Am I morally pure—what I see, what I think, what I do, where I go, what I listen to, what I say?

MY TONGUE

*Take my lips, and let them be
filled with messages from Thee.*

✷ Do the words that come out of my mouth reveal that my lips and tongue are fully surrendered to God?

✷ Do I habitually verbalize the goodness and greatness of God?

✷ Do I regularly ask the Lord to guard my tongue?

✷ Before I speak, do I ask the Lord what He wants me to say?

❋ Am I filling my mind and heart with the
Word of God, so that what comes out of my
mouth will be "messages from Him"?

❋ Do I speak words that are critical, unkind,
untrue, self-centered, rude, profane, or
unnecessary?

❋ Do I look for and take advantage of opportunities to give a verbal witness for Christ?

❋ Do I intentionally use my tongue to edify and
encourage others in their walk with God?

MY POSSESSIONS

Take my silver and my gold;
not a mite would I withhold.

❋ Do I treat any of my possessions as if they
were mine rather than God's?

❋ Do I give generously, sacrificially, and gladly to
the Lord's work and to others in need?

❋ Do I own anything that I would not be willing to part with if God were to take it from
me or ask me to give it to another?

❋ Am I a wise steward of the material
resources God has entrusted to me?

❋ Do I view God as my provider and the source of all my material possessions?

❋ Am I content with the material resources God has given me? If God should choose not to give me one thing more than what I already have, would I be satisfied with His provision?

❋ Do I give my tithes and offerings to the Lord before I pay my bills or spend my income?

❋ Do I become angry or upset if others are careless with "my" possessions?

My Mind

Take my intellect, and use
every power as Thou shalt choose.

❋ Am I "bringing every thought into captivity to the obedience of Christ" (2 Corinthians 10:5)?

❋ Am I disciplining my mind to get to know God and His Word better?

❋ Am I wasting my mind on worldly knowledge or pursuits that do not have eternal, spiritual value?

* Do I habitually think about things that are just, pure, lovely, of good report, virtuous, and praiseworthy (Philippians 4:8), rather than things that are unwholesome, negative, impure, or vain?

* Am I guarding the entrance of my mind from impure influences (e.g., books, magazines, movies, music, conversations)?

* Am I devoting my mental capacity to serving Christ and furthering His kingdom?

My Will

Take my will and make it Thine;
it shall be no longer mine.

* Do I consistently seek to know and to do the will of God in the practical, daily matters of life?

* When I read the Word of God (or hear it proclaimed), am I quick to say, "Yes, Lord" and to do what it says?

* Is there anything God has shown me to be His will that I have been neglecting or refusing to obey?

❋ Is there anything I know God wants me to do that I have not done/am not doing?

❋ Do I become resentful when things don't go my way? Do I have to have the last word in disagreements?

❋ Am I stubborn? Demanding? Controlling?

❋ Am I quick to respond in confession and repentance when the Holy Spirit convicts me of sin?

❋ Am I submissive to the human authorities God has placed over me (e.g., civil, church, home, work)?

MY AFFECTIONS

Take my heart; it is Thine own;
it shall be Thy royal throne.

❋ Am I moody? Temperamental? Hard to please?

❋ Do I love Christ and His kingdom more than this earth and its pleasures? Is there anything or anyone that I am more devoted to than Christ?

❋ Am I allowing Christ to reign and rule over my affections, my emotions, and my responses?

❋ Am I easily angered or provoked?

❋ Am I allowing anyone or anything other than Christ to control my emotions and responses?

❋ Are my desires, appetites, and longings under Christ's control?

❋ Am I in bondage to any earthly, fleshly, or sinful desires or appetites? Am I indulging or making provision for my fleshly desires (Romans 13:14)?

❋ Do I trust God's right to rule over the circumstances of my life?

My Relationships

Take my love; my Lord,
I pour at Thy feet its treasure store.

❋ Is it my desire and intent to love God with all my heart, above all earthly relationships? Do I enjoy and seek out the friendship of God as much as I do human friendships?

✳ Do I love God more than I love myself? Do I seek His interests, His reputation, and His pleasure above my own?

✳ Have I surrendered to God all my desires, rights, and expectations regarding my family?

✳ Am I willing to let God decide whether I am to be married and to whom?

✳ Have I surrendered the right to have a loving, godly mate?

✳ Am I willing to love my mate in a Christlike way, regardless of whether or not that love is reciprocated?

✳ Have I accepted God's decision to grant or withhold the blessing of children?

✳ Have I released my children to the Lord? Am I trying to control their lives? Am I willing for Him to call them and use them in His service—anywhere, in any way, regardless of the cost?

✳ Is there anyone that I "love" in a way that is not pure? Am I holding on to any friendships or relationships that God wants me to relinquish?

❊ Am I willing to sacrifice friendships, if necessary, in order to obey God and His call in my life?

❊ Am I willing to speak the truth in love to others about their spiritual condition, even if it means risking the loss of the relationship or my reputation?

MYSELF

*Take myself, and I will be
ever, only, all for Thee.*

❊ Have I surrendered all that I am and all that I have to God?

❊ Is there any part of myself—my plans, relationships, possessions, emotions, career, future—that I am knowingly holding back from God?

❊ Have I settled the issue that the ultimate purpose of my life is to please God and bring Him glory?

❊ Is it the intent of my heart, by His grace, to live the rest of my life wholly for Him and for His pleasure, rather than for myself and my pleasure?

MAKING IT EVEN MORE PERSONAL . . .

You may have expressed your desire to be fully surrendered to God many times before. Or you may just now be recognizing what it means to be totally surrendered to Him. Regardless, would you stop—right now, if possible—and slip to your knees before the Lord and pray, *O Lord, afresh this moment, I surrender every part of my being—all I am and all I have —to You.*

As you pray these next words, visualize the place where you are kneeling as an altar of sacrifice, and picture each part of yourself being offered up to God as a living sacrifice: *I consecrate to You my life . . . my time . . . my body . . . my tongue . . . my possessions . . . my mind . . . my will . . . my affections . . . my relationships . . . myself. Take me, have me, do with me as You please. I am Yours for this moment and forever. Please work out that surrender in my life—every day, in every matter, until I bow before You in eternity. Amen.*

NOTE

1. Frances Ridley Havergal, *Kept for the Master's Use* (Chicago: Moody, 1999 [reprt.]), 23.

THE PATTERN:
THE SURRENDERED SAVIOR

Dear Lord, You be the needle
and I be the thread.
You go first, and I will follow
wherever You may lead.

*

*

From the time I was a little girl and was first introduced to *The Shoemaker Who Gave India the Bible* (the story of missionary William Carey), I have had a voracious appetite for biographies of "Christian heroes." My heart has been deeply stirred by the stories of Hudson Taylor, George Mueller, Gladys Aylward, and others whose lives are portraits of complete consecration to Christ as Lord.

However, the pages of history do not contain any more moving and powerful picture of what it means to be surrendered to the will of God than that of the Lord Jesus Himself. From eternity past, through all of time, and through all of eternity future, Jesus' life was, is, and always will be, one of absolute surrender.

Before there was time, the Lord Jesus, though co-equal with the Father, willingly placed Himself under the authority of the Father. At the creation and throughout the unfolding of the Old Testament era, He was by His Father's side, delighting to join the Father in His work. He existed in perfect oneness with His Father, never willing anything contrary to the Father's will.

SATAN ATTEMPTED TO GET JESUS TO SURRENDER TO HIS CONTROL.

"I Have Come to Do Your Will"

When Jesus left heaven to come to earth, He had one purpose in mind:

"I have come down from heaven not to do my will but to do the will of him who sent me."
—John 6:38 NIV

Then I said, "Here I am . . . I have come to do your will, O God."
—Hebrews 10:7 NIV

We consider it remarkable when a human being fully surrenders his or her agenda and will to the will of God—probably because such an individual is so rare. But as we have seen, in light of who God is and who we are, such surrender is completely reasonable. What makes the attitude of the Lord Jesus so astounding is that He is *God*. For Him to surrender His will to that of the Father can only be explained in terms of utter selflessness, trust, humility, and deep devotion to His Father.

Throughout His years here on earth, Jesus maintained this posture of surrender to God. Virtually the only insight we are given into Jesus' life from age twelve till He reached manhood is that He was obedient to His parents (Luke 2:51). That obedience to human authorities was an expression of His surrender to the will of God.

Before He began His earthly ministry, Jesus endured a period of intense temptation in the desert. What was the underlying issue that Satan used to tempt Jesus? It was this matter of control.

As he had done with the man and the woman in the garden of Eden four thousand years earlier, Satan attempted to get Jesus to surrender to his control. And as with the first couple, he started by appealing to Jesus' physical appetites—*you decide what to eat and when*. Though Jesus had not eaten in forty days, He refused to operate apart from the direction of His Father, even in a seemingly insignificant matter.

In his final volley, Satan offered to give Jesus "all the kingdoms of the world and their splendor" (something that was not his to give, for that all belongs to God!), if only "you will bow down and worship me" (Matthew 4:8–9 NIV).

Adam and Eve had failed essentially that same test. Offered an opportunity to control their own lives, they had bowed down and worshiped the one whose sole intent is to usurp the throne of God.

Jesus knew that if He conceded even an iota of control to Satan, He would be rejecting the kingdom and control of God. He understood that that is the essence of sin; it is what separates God from man, and it is what accounts for all the misery in the history of the world.

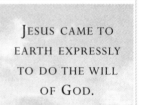

JESUS CAME TO EARTH EXPRESSLY TO DO THE WILL OF GOD.

Jesus acknowledged only one King and was fully surrendered to the will of His heavenly Father; therefore, He would not for a moment concede control to the Father's archenemy. He would not bow before any other so-called king; He would not worship anyone other than God. He would not indulge His human desires for food or comfort or gain, if to do so required Him to operate outside His Father's will.

Jesus came to earth expressly to do the will of God, which required that He offer up His body as a sacrifice. Never for a single moment did He ever resist the will of His Father. Never was there a hint

of a power struggle between Father and Son—never
a battle for control—just complete, glad surrender.
To demonstrate that surrender, the Lord Jesus took
upon Himself "the form of a bond-servant." Then, in
the ultimate display of relinquishing control, "He
humbled Himself by becoming obedient to the
point of death" (Philippians 2:7–8 NASB).

The Supreme Surrender

"But what about Gethsemane?" you say. "Didn't
Jesus struggle against the will of God as He faced the
cross?" To the contrary, next to the cross itself,
Gethsemane is the supreme illustration of Jesus' surrender while here on this earth.

Shortly before going to Gethsemane to pray, Jesus
predicted His imminent death. Then He said, "Now
my heart is troubled, and what shall I say? 'Father,
save me from this hour'? *No, it was for this very reason I came to this hour.* Father, glorify your name!"
(John 12:27–28 NIV, italics added).

Before He ever set foot in the garden of
Gethsemane, Jesus had settled the issue; indeed, the
issue had been settled before He ever set foot on this
planet. In eternity past, He had surrendered Himself
to the will of God—to become the Sin-Bearer for all
mankind. When Jesus knelt in the garden and
"offered up prayers and petitions with loud cries and

tears to the one who could save him from death"
(Hebrews 5:7 NIV), He was not expressing resistance
to the will of God; rather, He was expressing *full surrender* to the will of God.

The anguish the Lord Jesus experienced as He
sweated drops of blood was that He who had never
once disobeyed His Father, He who loved His Father
and had been by His Father's side for all of eternity
(Proverbs 8:30), He who delighted to do the will of
His Father (Psalm 40:8), He who "loved righteousness and hated lawlessness" (Hebrews 1:9)—was
about to *become sin*—the very thing He knew His
Father hated! The surrendered Son of God was
about to take on Himself all the cumulative, com-
pounded resistance and rebellion of all humans who
had ever lived or ever would live on this planet.

So He cried out, in effect, "O Father, my Holy
Father, I've lived to please You. And because I love
You, if it's possible, let this cup pass from Me so that
I will not have to be sin, so that I will not have to be
separated from You."

The writer of Hebrews tells us that when Jesus
cried out, "he was heard *because of his reverent submission*" (5:7 NIV, italics added). That submission was seen
as He prayed in the garden: "Not My will, but Yours be
done." What was He saying? *I delight to do Your will.
That's all that matters. Father, I surrender to Your control.*

Bow the Head

Jesus left the garden under arrest. Not many hours later, He laid down His life on the cross. The Scripture is clear that no man took His life from Him. John's account of the crucifixion gives us a significant detail that is not included in the other gospels. We are told that after Jesus drank the vinegar, He said, "'It is finished.' With that, *he bowed his head* and gave up his spirit" (19:30 NIV, italics added).

Can you see it? *He bowed His head.* He didn't just slump over. He bowed His head. In that final moment of His life, He performed one last, powerful, volitional act—He bowed His head. He

Our Savior will forever be a surrendered servant.

chose the pathway of surrender. "He was heard because of his reverent submission." He surrendered—willingly, freely gave up His life—so you and I could inherit eternal life.

What a God! What a Savior!

And what a calling! As Christ's surrender took Him to the cross, so our surrender will always take us to the cross. Every time your flesh or mine crosses the will of God and we choose to *bow the head* in surrender to the Spirit of God, our will is crucified and Christ is exalted as Lord. So . . .

❈ When your flesh wants to watch that raunchy TV program, and the Spirit says, "Cast off the works of darkness" (Romans 13:12), see it as an opportunity to consciously, volitionally *bow your head* and surrender to God.

❈ When your flesh wants to lash out in anger, and the Spirit says, "Clothe [yourself] with compassion, kindness, humility, gentleness and patience. Bear with each other . . ." (Colossians 3:12–13 NIV), *bow your head* and surrender to God.

❈ When your flesh wants to pass along a critical report about another believer, and the Spirit says, "Speak evil of no one" (Titus 3:2), *bow your head* and surrender to God.

❈ When your flesh is tempted to complain about your circumstances, and the Spirit says, "In everything give thanks" (1 Thessalonians 5:18), *bow your head* and surrender to God.

❈ When your flesh rises up against an authority you think is being unreasonable, and the Spirit says, "Submit [yourself] for the Lord's sake to every authority" (1 Peter 2:13 NIV), *bow your head* and surrender to God.

※ When your flesh wants to wound that mate or child or friend who has wounded you, and the Spirit says, "Repay no one evil for evil" (Romans 12:17), *bow your head* and surrender to God.

※ When your flesh wants to say something that makes you look good, and the Spirit says, "Let another man praise you, and not your own mouth" (Proverbs 27:2), *bow your head* and surrender to God.

※ When your flesh wants to indulge in sexual fantasies, and the Spirit says, "Blessed are the pure in heart" (Matthew 5:8) and "Take captive every thought to make it obedient to Christ" (2 Corinthians 10:5 NIV), *bow your head* and surrender to God.

※ When your flesh wants to hoard your financial resources out of fear of the future, and the Spirit says, "He who gives to the poor will not lack" (Proverbs 28:27), *bow your head* and surrender to God.

※ When your flesh wants to shade the truth to protect your reputation, and the Spirit says, "Each one speak truth with his neighbor" (Ephesians 4:25), *bow your head* and surrender to God.

❋ When your flesh wants to eat in excess, and
the Spirit says, "Whether you eat or drink . . .
do all to the glory of God" (1 Corinthians
10:31), *bow your head* and surrender to God.

Every time you and I bow our heads in acceptance of and surrender to the will of God, we
embrace the cross and we manifest to the world the
heart of Christ who bowed His head to the will of
His Father.

ETERNALLY SURRENDERED

We have seen that from eternity past, through His
incarnation, in His earthly life and ministry, and in
His death on the cross, the Lord Jesus was a surrendered servant. Yet our portrait is not quite finished.
Did you realize that for all of eternity, our Savior will
forever be a surrendered servant?

Luke's gospel paints a picture that never fails to
move me; it describes what will happen when Jesus,
our Master, returns for His faithful servants: "I tell
you the truth, he will dress himself to serve, will have
them recline at the table *and will come and wait on
them*" (12:37 NIV, italics added). Can you fathom
that? *The King and Lord of the universe* will put on a
servant's uniform and will come and wait on *us*? It
takes my breath away.

Now let's stand back and watch as the Master Artist adds the final strokes to this exquisite picture of surrender. We see the consummation of that cosmic battle for control that has been intensifying since Lucifer first asserted his will against the will of God:

> *And there were loud voices in heaven, saying, "The kingdoms of this world have become the kingdoms of our Lord and of His Christ, and He shall reign forever and ever!"*
>
> —Revelation 11:15b

And so, the surrendered servant takes His place with His Father on the highest throne in heaven and earth, to rule forever as the Sovereign Lord.

But wait! (As I read these passages, I'm reminded of the final movement of a symphony that progresses from one triumphant, climactic finale to another.)

One more scene completes this portrait. In keeping with the character and heart of our Savior-King, His very last action is not best described with loud, crashing cymbals of majestic conquest, but with the rich, lush, sweeping sounds of . . . *surrender:*

> *Then the end will come, when [Christ] hands over the kingdom to God the Father after he has destroyed all dominion, authority and power. For he must reign until he has put all his enemies under his feet. . . . When he*

has done this, then the Son himself will be made subject to him who put everything under him, so that
God may be all in all.

—1 Corinthians 15:24–25, 28 NIV
(emphasis added)

When all is said and done, the conquering King
will turn over to His Father all the kingdoms He has
overcome—all the spoils of war. And then, once
again, as time gives way to eternity, the Son of God,
the Almighty, sovereign Creator and Redeemer, the
Lord of heaven and earth, will bow His head in a
final, magnificent act of surrender.

MAKING IT PERSONAL . . .

❋ "Your attitude should be the same as that of
Christ Jesus" (Philippians 2:5 NIV). How does
your attitude reflect the heart of the Lord
Jesus? How is it different than His?

❋ What is an issue you are currently facing in
which you need to *bow your head?*

YES, LORD!
BOWING THE KNEE

Say "No" to self;
"Yes" to Jesus every time.

WILLIAM BORDEN[1]

A number of years ago, I was asked to speak to several hundred college students at a conference held between Christmas and New Year's Day. Ordinarily, I do not take speaking engagements over the Christmas holidays; it's the one time of year I don't have to travel, and I look forward to being at home. Although I did not want to make this trip, I felt the Lord wanted me to surrender my desires, so I bowed my will (somewhat reluctantly, I'll admit) and agreed to go.

As I spoke to those students about total surrender, I confessed the emotions I had struggled with in coming to the conference. I shared that, in my humanness, I would have preferred to stay in my house, relax, and look at the river outside my home, rather than having to travel and speak during the holidays, but that it had come down to an issue of surrender.

As I had been preparing to speak, I had a sense that God wanted many of those students to surrender their lives to vocational Christian service. At the close of the message, I told the students what was on my heart and asked them to consider what God might be saying to them and then simply to bow the knee and say, *Yes, Lord.*

> AM I SEEKING TO KNOW AND FOLLOW THE WILL OF GOD IN *EVERY* AREA OF MY LIFE?

Two years later, I received a letter from a young woman who had attended that conference. She was writing to express what God had done in her heart that weekend. At the time she had been a junior in college, preparing for a career in advertising.

She recalled, "When you said you believed God was calling many of us to devote our lives to Christian service, I looked around wondering who you could be talking about—knowing it certainly couldn't be me!" But that day God planted a seed in her heart; she began to sense God's call to surrender her career plans and devote her life to the kingdom of Christ. She wanted me to know that she was in the process of raising her financial support to join the full-time staff of a student ministry (where she is still serving today).

I was particularly moved by her closing words: "I'm so glad you didn't choose to sit in your house and look at your river that New Year's holiday, but that you surrendered to God's call in your life."

In retrospect, I'm glad too. But I can't help thinking of other times when I have been slow to surrender to the will of God, and wondering how many more lives He might have touched in significant ways if I had been quicker to bow the knee and say, *Yes, Lord.*

CALLING HIM "LORD"

What would surrender to God's control look like for you? I asked a number of friends to share a significant point of surrender they had faced in their walk with God. They identified a variety of issues, including the surrender of:

* Personal possessions

* Spending habits

* Personal opinions (e.g., about how my church should be run)

* Children leaving home

* Schedule and time (e.g., to be a stay-at-home mom or to homeschool children)

⁎ Health and physical concerns

⁎ Addictive habits

⁎ The right to control or change a mate

⁎ Loss of parents through death

⁎ Home and comfort (e.g., to move and serve in a ministry)

The specific issues that God identifies in your life may be similar or different. The question you must answer is, *Am I seeking to know and follow the will of God in* every *area of my life?* The fact is, many professing Christians go through life making decisions and responding to circumstances while rarely considering, "What does *God* want me to do? What does the Scripture say about this?"

> WE CANNOT CALL HIM *LORD* AND THEN PROCEED TO RUN OUR OWN LIVES.

Jesus put it this way: "Why do you call me 'Lord, Lord,' and do not do what I say?" (Luke 6:46 NIV). In other words, "Why do you claim that I am in charge of your life, but you run your life as if you were in charge? You don't ask Me what I want you to do, and even when you know what I want you to do, you still insist on doing it your way!"

To call Him *Lord* means to say *Yes*—to His will, His Word, and His ways. We cannot call Him *Lord* and then proceed to run our own lives.

You say, "If I live a surrendered life, does that mean I'll end up on the mission field . . . or have to quit my job . . . or bring my parents to live in our home . . . or live alone all my life?" Maybe. Maybe not. In a sense, it doesn't really matter. What does matter is saying *Yes, Lord.* Then you will have grace to do the will of God—whatever it is—and joy as you do it!

Surrendering to God may mean being happily married for half a century. Or being faithful in a difficult marriage to an unbeliever. Or being widowed and left to raise young children. Or never marrying. What matters is saying *Yes, Lord.*

It may mean parenting many children. Or few children. Or no children. What matters is, *How many children does God want you to have?*

It may mean you make lots of money and use it for the glory of God. Or that only your essential needs are met and you choose to be content with little.

It may mean you own a lovely, large home and use it to bless and serve others. Or it may mean you live in a two-room efficiency in a Third World country where you spend years translating the Scripture for those who have never heard the Word of God. Regardless, what matters is saying *Yes, Lord.*

Total surrender to Christ as Lord simply means submitting every detail and dimension of our lives to His sovereign, loving rule.

BOWING THE KNEE

For years, I have made it a practice to kneel before the Lord at least once a day, as a physical expression of my desire to surrender my will to His will.

To be totally surrendered to God means to bow the knee before a Sovereign Lord. It means to say *Yes* to God . . .

* *Yes* to His choices for your life—even when they don't seem comfortable or convenient

* *Yes* to difficult or painful circumstances that you cannot understand or change

* *Yes* to everything that is revealed in His Word

* *Yes* to His plans, His purposes, and His priorities

* *Yes* to the human authorities He has placed in your life

* *Yes* to His disciplines

❊ *Yes* to His control over your appetites, your
  body, your time, your relationships, your
  future—everything

To some, that type of surrender might seem to be
bondage; but those who have bowed the knee—those
who have laid down their arms and waved the white
flag of surrender—know that it is the only pathway to
true freedom. And with that surrender comes a host of
blessings that cannot be experienced any other way:
the grace to obey God, release from having to run our
own world, the peace of God, unexplainable fullness
of joy, and greater fruitfulness than we ever dreamed
possible.

I have seen this so many times in my own life that
I often look back and wonder, *Why did I ever resist
the will of God?!*

"Please, Not Me, Lord!"

Someone has said that the will of God is exactly
what we would choose if we knew what God knows.
The problem is, we don't know what God knows—
which is why we so often find it difficult to embrace
His will and why we must learn to "trust and obey."

As I look back over my life thus far, I am in awe at
the beauty and magnificence of His sovereign plan,
and the intricate, loving way that He orchestrates the

details of our lives—if we will let Him. Every time we step out in faith to surrender to His will—each time we say *Yes* to God—we move into a realm of greater blessing and fruitfulness.

I'll never forget the time I was first challenged to consider starting a daily radio program for women. From the outset, I had multiple objections to the idea, and was quick to list them to the Lord and others. Some of those reservations were practical—I knew virtually nothing about broadcasting and felt utterly inadequate and incapable of taking on such a responsibility.

Other hurdles were more personal—I was in my early forties and was wishing for a more settled life than I had experienced over more than twenty years of itinerant ministry. In my mind, accepting this responsibility would mean working harder and having less "free time" than ever; it would mean relinquishing any thought of anonymity, of privacy, or of a "normal" life—things I longed to enjoy. I remember thinking, *This would mean having no life of my own!*

Then my heart was pierced. From the time I was a little girl, I had recognized God's ownership of my life and had acknowledged that my life was not my own. Yet here I was trying to protect and preserve part of it for myself.

Years earlier, I had signed that blank contract,

giving my life wholly to God to be used for His purposes; now that God was filling in the details, I knew that I could not take it back. Once again, I had to come to a fresh point of surrender to the will of God, regardless of what that might mean or what the cost might be. Finally, I said, "*Yes, Lord.* I am Your servant. You know my weaknesses, my fears, and my personal desires. But I will embrace whatever You reveal to be Your will in this matter."

Once I came to that point of surrender, God began to ignite faith in my heart—faith that He would enable me to do whatever He called me to do, in spite of my personal limitations and inadequacies.

MY FRIEND, *IT'S ALL ABOUT COMPLETE SURRENDER.*

God's call in your life will probably look different than it does in mine—or in anyone else's. Regardless of the details, He asks simply that we bow the knee and say, *Yes, Lord.*

The pathway of surrender is not always an easy one. On occasion, I have found myself in some pretty turbulent waters, as a result of saying *Yes* to God. There have been points when it seemed like my little boat was going to capsize. But I have learned that there really is no safer place to be than in His will. And in the midst of the storms, I have found *joy*—indescribable joy. And blessings more than I can number—blessings to be enjoyed here and now and the anticipation of eternal blessings that I cannot begin to fathom now. It really is true that "there's no other way to be happy in Jesus, but to trust and obey."[2]

"ANNIE, IT'S COMPLETE SURRENDER"

In the 1924 Paris Olympics, a twenty-two-year-old Scottish athlete made headlines when he determined to say *No* to self and *Yes* to God. Eric Liddell made a decision that would have been unthinkable for most—to drop out of his best event, the hundred-yard dash, because the qualifying heats were being held on a Sunday. While his competitors were participating in the heats, Liddell was preaching a sermon at a nearby church.

Subsequently, Liddell entered himself in the 400-yard dash, a race for which he had not trained. He ran the race, finishing five yards ahead of his nearest competitor and setting a new world record. However, that Olympic gold medal, earned under such extraordinary circumstances, was far from Eric Liddell's greatest accomplishment.

His obedience to God in Paris was just one of a lifelong series of surrenders that earned Eric the applause of heaven. After his Olympic triumph, he returned to China where he had been raised, to serve as a missionary. In 1943, he was interned in a Japanese concentration camp in China, where he continued to serve God and joyfully ministered to his fellow prisoners. While still in the camp, Liddell suffered a brain tumor that ravaged his body and left him partially paralyzed.

On February 21, 1945, Eric lay on a hospital bed, struggling to breathe and moving in and out of consciousness. Finally, he went into a convulsion; the nurse who had been by his side took him into her arms as he managed to breathe his final words: "Annie," he said, his voice barely audible, *"it's complete surrender."*

Eric Liddell slipped into a coma and then into eternity, where the bond servant bowed the knee before the Master he loved so dearly and for whom he had labored so faithfully.

MAKING IT PERSONAL . . .

My friend, *it's all about complete surrender.* Whatever the issue may be for you, however trivial or daunting that issue may seem, whatever the price, whatever your fears, however foolish you may feel or look, wherever that surrender may lead you . . . right here, right now, will you bow the knee? Relinquish control. Let Him have His way. Say simply, *Yes, Lord; I surrender all.*

NOTES

1. Dick Bohrer, *Bill Borden: The Finished Course—the Unfinished Task* (Chicago: Moody, 1984), 41–42.

2. John H. Sammis, "Trust and Obey."

SURRENDER
Discussion Guide

As You Begin

The whole idea of surrendering to someone else's control runs counter to the prevailing mindset of our culture—we don't want anyone telling us what to do—we want to be in control of our own lives! But paradoxically, we are never truly free until we have fully surrendered ourselves to the Word and will of God.

The thought of delving into this topic may cause some apprehension in your heart, but as you engage in this study, you will encounter a wise, loving, merciful Lord who can be trusted.

The more fully you relinquish yourself to Him, the more you will discover that He has your best interests at heart and that His will truly is "good, acceptable, and perfect" (see Romans 12:2).

May your deepest heart's desire become that of the Savior who lifted His eyes heavenward, even as

He faced the cross, and said, *"I delight to do Your will, my God."*

TIPS FOR GROUP LEADERS

Open and close each meeting by praying together. Ask the Holy Spirit to guide you through the Word, to help you be real with one another, and to bring about any needed change in each heart.

Seek to lead by example. You can serve your group best by modeling a surrendered heart—by being quick to say, *Yes, Lord,* and encouraging others to do the same.

Some of the questions in this discussion guide call for a level of transparency and openness that many people are not accustomed to. Encourage the members of your group to respect each other's privacy by not discussing others' contributions outside of this group. Remind them that God is patient and gracious with us as He conforms us to the image of His Son, and that we need to extend the same patience and grace toward each other.

This discussion guide is designed to be used in a variety of contexts—from small groups to Sunday school classes. Feel free to direct the discussion based on the size of your group and the allotted time. Avoid rabbit trails into secondary or unrelated issues. However, don't feel pressured to get through all the questions each time you meet.

Depending on your available time and the size and openness of your group, you may end up only discussing two or three questions. The goal is to grow together in your understanding of God and His ways and to experience individually and as a group the reality of the message of this book.

Encourage each member to read the chapter and to complete the "Making It Personal" section found at the end of most chapters, prior to your group meeting. If possible, they should also preview and be prepared to discuss the questions found in this discussion guide.

Keep your group centered on the truth of the gospel: We are *all* sinners in need of a Savior. Help your members steer clear of self-righteous responses to the confessions of others in the group and from condemnation about their own performance by pointing them to the One who is both the author and perfecter of their faith (Hebrews 12:2 NIV).

Introduction

Opening Prayer

Turn to the prayer from *The Valley of Vision*, found at the beginning of *Surrender*. Start your time together by reading this wonderful expression of trust in the will of God. You may choose to read as a group in unison or have one or more read aloud while others listen.

Getting Started

Sometimes we dig our heels in about things that appear foolish in hindsight. Describe a situation where you held out for something that you realized in retrospect was misguided or didn't make sense. What finally convinced you to "surrender" your position?

Going Deeper

1. The introduction distinguishes between our *initial* surrender to Christ as our Lord and Savior (or conversion), and a *lifetime* of surrender (or consecration), as we learn to live out the implications of that initial surrender. Briefly describe the setting and circumstances of your conversion —your initial surrender to Christ.

2. *"The fully surrendered life is intended to be—and can be—the norm for every one of God's children"* (p. 25). Do you agree with this statement? From your perspective, is the "fully surrendered life" the "norm" for most of the believers you know?

3. Review and discuss the four reasons suggested in this chapter for why professing Christians may have areas of their life that are "unsurrendered" to God (pp. 22–24). Which of those four scenarios do you think are most common among "believers" whom you have observed? Have several in the group share an illustration out of their own lives of one of those scenarios.

4. *"Do you fear what a lifestyle of full surrender might cost you?"* (p. 25). What fears might people have about fully surrendering every aspect of their lives to God? What fears have you experienced at one point or another in relation to full surrender?

5. *"The truth is that resistance is far more costly than surrender"* (p. 26). What might we stand to lose by holding out on God?

6. Share out of your personal experience either the cost of resisting God on some particular point or the blessing you have experienced through relinquishing control of some area of your life to the Lord.

7. In many ways, surrender is an act of trust. You drop your defenses and trust your opponent will honor the terms of your surrender. The pardon given by President Marcos of the Philippines to Hiroo Onoda is a picture of the pardon we are given by God when we repent. What do you know about the heart and ways of God that should make it easier to trust Him and relinquish control to Him?

A Word of Encouragement

As you read the introduction and considered your own spiritual condition, your heart may have been pricked with the thought that perhaps you have never been truly regenerated (born again). You may have made a profession of faith; others may think of you as a "good Christian." But you have never "waved the white flag" and surrendered your life to Christ.

Don't try to talk yourself out of (or let anyone else talk you out of!) any conviction that God may be bringing to your heart. Seek out your pastor or another mature Christian for care and counsel. It may be that the tug of conviction you are experiencing is the doorway to the great joy of true salvation!

This could be a God-designed moment for you to repent of your sins and receive His forgiveness —please don't delay this important conversation!

For Next Time

"Could it be that there are some issues on which you are reserving the right to control your own life?" (p. 22). As you read and discussed the introduction to *Surrender,* God may have brought to mind specific areas in your life that are not fully surrendered to His control. Record these areas in a personal journal. Ask God to help you see these issues as He does and express your desire for every area of your life to be under His control.

Grace Note

In the life of a believer, the Holy Spirit brings conviction, not condemnation. Conviction is sweet because it is accompanied by the promise of grace to change. Condemnation brings on guilt (usually heaped on by the Enemy) that we will never measure up to God's demands. Without being born again and trusting in God's power to change us, that would be true. Don't let condemnation rob you of the joy of this journey toward change!

Remember: *"Our God abounds in mercy and grace; He is willing to offer a full and complete pardon to those who lay down their weapons"* (p. 26).

Chapter One:
THE BATTLE
FOR CONTROL

Getting Started

Has anyone in your group ever served in combat or had a friend or relative who did? Describe your experience of being in battle (or what you have heard from your loved one). What did you learn about how to wage and win a battle?

Going Deeper

1. What evidences do you see of nature being "surrendered" to God's control? Why do you think God gives human beings the freedom to submit to or to resist His control? What limitations has He placed on that freedom, both here and now, as well as ultimately?

2. Did you relate to any of the fictitious scenarios at the beginning of this chapter (pp. 31–33)? What is one example of a recurring battle you have experienced in your Christian life? How could that struggle actually be a battle for control?

3. *"Count on it—the very points on which you refuse to surrender will become 'enemies' that rule over you"* (p. 42). What are some practical examples of how this principle could take place in someone's life?

4. What is one area of your life that has ended up ruling you as a "tyrant" (either in the past or in the present) because of a lack of surrender to God?

5. Lynda's testimony (pp. 40–44) illustrates the truth of Romans 6:16—"Do you not know that to whom you present yourselves slaves to obey, you are that one's slaves whom you obey, whether of sin leading to death, or of obedience leading to righteousness?"

Share one particular area of your life where you have experienced (or currently experience) a sense of being *enslaved* to sin or ungodly desires. How could surrender to God set you free from that slavery?

6. Take time to pray for each other in relation to any specific battles for control or surrender issues that have been shared.

For Next Time

With regard to any "unsurrendered" areas you have identified in your life, reflect on the effects of being enslaved to these areas. List the bad fruits of being submitted to these desires, so you can see more clearly the cost of your lack of surrender.

Grace Note

Surrender brings peace and a foretaste of the "paradise restored" that every believer will enjoy one day in heaven. You can begin to enjoy those benefits now by saying yes to God. As the familiar song says, "There's no other way to be happy in Jesus, but to *trust and obey.*"

Chapter Two:
THE TERMS
OF CHRISTIAN
SURRENDER

Getting Started

Has anyone in your group ever visited
Appomattox? If so, what did you learn during your
visit? What struck you about the illustration in this
chapter of Robert E. Lee's surrender at Appomattox
(pp. 49–52)? What parallels did you see to
Christian surrender?

Lee's surrender was a "decisive moment" that
changed the course of the Civil War and assured its
ultimate outcome. What does that illustrate about
the importance of a "decisive moment" of surrender in our relationship with God?

Going Deeper

1. *"The person who has never acknowledged
Christ's right to rule over his life has no basis for
assurance of salvation. . . . Surrender to the will of
God is a mark of the truly converted"* (p. 54).

What part does surrender have in true Christian
conversion? What concerns does this raise about

our message and methods as we seek to share the gospel with unbelievers?

2. How would you define or describe *unconditional* surrender? What does that mean for a believer? What might *conditional* surrender look like? Why is it unacceptable for a child of God?

3. How would you distinguish between an *initial point* of surrender to Christ, and an ongoing, *lifelong process* of surrender in a believer's life? What is the connection between the two? Why are both important? How can an initial, unconditional surrender to the lordship of Christ simplify subsequent points of surrender along the way? (Think of the illustration of the dieter on p. 58!)

4. Share a situation you have faced recently that required you to freshly affirm and live out your surrender to the will of God. It may have been a choice to obey God's Word or the prompting of His Spirit on a simple, everday matter, or it may have been a more major point of surrender.

5. Why might some consider John and Betty Stam's surrender and sacrifice to be a net loss? How would you evaluate their surrender from an eternal perspective?

6. Why might the concept of "signing a blank contract" for your life and letting God fill in the

details seem risky or frightening to some? Why is it really not risky at all? What do we stand to lose by unconditional surrender to God? What do we stand to gain?

7. Discuss any reservations or fears you have about signing your life over to God, or share what you have learned or experienced that has relieved your fears of that kind of surrender.

For Next Time

If you haven't already done so, write out a prayer expressing your heart's intent to be wholly surrendered to Christ. Then date and sign your "contract" with the Lord.

Grace Note

There are three wonderful prayers from saints of old included in this chapter (pp. 60–62). If time permits, read these aloud in your group. If not, read them aloud during your personal time with the Lord over the next week.

Chapter Three:
A HOLE
IN THE EAR

Getting Started

Has anyone in your group traveled abroad or spent time ministering internationally? If so, did you observe anything in the lives of the believers in that part of the world that particularly impressed you or struck you as different than American Christianity?

Going Deeper

1. Discuss the difference between *commitment* and *surrender* as Josef Tson explains it (pp. 70–71). Which term do you think better characterizes contemporary Christianity in the West? What are the implications of adopting one perspective or the other?

2. Discuss the difference (as Josef Tson and Webster's dictionary explain it) between a servant and a slave. Which term would the majority of believers in our culture be more comfortable using to describe our relationships to Christ? Why?

3. What are the implications of the fact in the Greek Bible that one never *serves* God but rather one *slaves* to God (pp. 71–72)?

4. How does the ceremony of joyful slavery found in Exodus 21 illustrate a believer's relationship to God? How was this Old Testament picture fulfilled in Christ?

5. What are some of the "requirements" of being Christ's bondslave that you have found difficult at one time or another?

6. What are some of the privileges, joys, and blessings you have experienced as a result of being His bondslave?

7. Close your time by reading the words of David Livingstone (p. 67) and Mary of Nazareth (p. 81). Then pray together and express your desire to make these words your own.

For Next Time

A man or a woman with "a hole in the ear" is easily identifiable to others. Are there any relationships or circumstances in which you are tempted to, in effect, "cover up" that hole? Prayerfully consider those situations, and ask the Holy Spirit to show you the motivations and cravings of your heart that compel such a reaction—and then after asking His forgiveness, ask for the grace to change.

Grace Note

As you consider this idea of being a slave to Christ, meditate on the truths found in Psalm 40. Jesus fulfilled this prophetic statement through His atoning death; He is the first and foremost bond-slave to God. He fulfilled the prophetic picture of Exodus 21 in His joyful submission to a gracious and loving Master!

Chapter Four:
THE WHOLE OF OUR LIVES

Getting Started

Probably few if any in your group can identify with the passion for Communism described at the beginning of this chapter. But you have probably seen that kind of fanatical devotion to some cause or endeavor (other than the kingdom of God). What have you observed and what were the results?

Going Deeper

1. How did the young Communist's letter to his fiancée impress you? How does his level of devotion to the Communist cause compare to the average Christian's devotion to Christ and His kingdom? How does it compare to your own values and priorities?

2. What were the characteristics of a burnt offering in the Jewish worship system? How did Christ fulfill that Old Testament picture? How does that picture help us understand what it means to be a true follower of Jesus Christ? How

is the sacrifice of our lives *different* than the Old Testament burnt offerings?

3. How does marriage illustrate the twofold aspect of surrender (an initial point, followed by an ongoing, lifetime process)?

4. Between the different members of your group, share some specific sacrifices you can recall God asking you to make—ranging from "twenty-five-cent pieces" to perhaps much larger sacrifices. Would you agree that, regardless of their size, *"the sacrifices God asks of us are never pointless"* (p. 96)?

5. Have you ever felt that something God was asking of you seemed unreasonable? What perspective does Romans 12:1 give to those sacrifices? Why do you think Paul used the Greek word *logikos* to describe the offering up of ourselves to God as a living sacrifice? How does Christ's sacrifice for us affect the way we view our sacrifices for Him?

6. What might it mean for you this week to offer yourself as a "living sacrifice" to God?

For Next Time

Reread Helen Roseveare's description of what it means to be a living sacrifice (pp. 97–98). Then try writing your own description of what it means to be a living sacrifice.

Grace Note

Don't forget the accent and emphasis of Romans 12:1 . . . "in view of God's mercy" (NIV). That's where the Holy Spirit started as He inspired the apostle Paul to write, and that is where we are to start. If you are wrestling with discouragement or fear, remember that surrender is always done "in view of God's mercy."

Chapter Five:
FACING
OUR FEARS

Getting Started

This chapter describes the "going but not knowing" aspect of surrender in Abraham's life. Some in your group have also probably undertaken such a "journey"—stepping out in faith without knowing precisely what lay ahead. Have one or more individuals share their story.

Going Deeper

1. Review the four fears addressed in this chapter in relation to surrendering everything to God. Is it wrong to have those fears?

2. Share an instance in which you experienced one of these fears in relation something God was asking you to do. Discuss as a group what promise(s) of God could have counteracted your fear in that situation.

3. What is the role of faith in helping us face our natural fears regarding the will of God? How can we grow in our faith? Why is it so important

that we know the promises and the character of God if we're going to trust Him?

4. In addition to "going not knowing," there's also the test of "waiting not receiving." Abraham experienced both. *"For more than twenty-five years, [Abraham] didn't have a shred of visible evidence that God's promises would be fulfilled"* (pp. 109–10).

Is there some matter on which you have been waiting on the Lord for what seems like a very long time? What has helped you to continue trusting God? What additional encouragement can others in the group offer from God's Word?

5. The word *Hebrew* means "stranger" or "alien." In what sense is every child of God a "Hebrew"? Can you think of a verse or passage in the New Testament that supports that concept?

6. "Trust or tyranny. *That is the option.* Trust *the promises of God—which will free you to live joy-fully under His loving Lordship—or live under the* tyranny *of that which you will not surrender"* (p. 115).

Encourage one or more in your group to share how failing to trust the promises of God caused them to resist surrender on a specific matter and resulted in living under the tyranny of that very thing.

7. *"Isn't that the heart of the matter for every child of God? Can you trust Me?"* (p. 121). Close your meeting with a time of prayer. Thank God for His character and His promises; express your trust in Him; ask Him to give you grace to face your fears and to fully surrender to Him any areas of life where you may have been afraid to say, *"Yes, Lord."*

For Next Time

Look for several verses that address the fear(s) you most related to in this chapter. You may want to post a visible reminder of these verses in your kitchen, on your bathroom mirror, on your dashboard, or your screen saver—wherever you are likely to encounter this truth consistently in your daily life.

Grace Note

Our loving God is not unmindful of our fears, tests, and trials. The loving reassurance He extended to Abram echoes throughout time to us today: "Do not be afraid, Abram. I am your shield, your exceedingly great reward" (Genesis 15:1). Whatever we surrender is *more* than matched by the exceedingly great reward of knowing God!

Chapter Six:
LIVING THE
SURRENDERED LIFE

Getting Started

"It's one thing to have an emotional experience at a Christian gathering where you are inspired and challenged to surrender control of everything to God. It's another matter to live out that surrender once the emotion of the moment has passed—when the bus gets home from the conference . . . when you lose your job and the bills keep coming . . . when you find out you're expecting your fifth child in seven years . . . when your mate is diagnosed with a terminal illness" (pp. 126–27). Describe such an occasion or experience in your life.

Going Deeper

Talk through each of the ten categories in this chapter (based on Frances Havergal's hymn "Take My Life and Let it Be"). (If time does not permit you to go through all of them, as a group select several to review.) What does it mean for each of these areas of our lives to be consecrated to God? Share any specific questions you found particularly challenging or convicting as you read this chapter.

1. My Life
2. My Time
3. My Body
4. My Tongue
5. My Possessions
6. My Mind
7. My Will
8. My Affections
9. My Relationships
10. Myself

For Next Time

Select one category from this chapter that you feel prompted to focus on between now and your next meeting. Each day, review the questions in that category that will help remind you of areas where you need a deeper surrender to the Lord.

If you haven't walked through the exercise recommended on p. 139, take time to do that this week.

Grace Note

Meditate on Frances Havergal's quote at the beginning of this chapter: *"Full consecration may be in one sense the act of a moment and in another the work of a lifetime. It must be complete to be real, and yet—if real—it is always incomplete. Consecration is a point of rest and yet a perpetual progression."* This thought should both motivate and encourage us to press on in the matter of full surrender to God.

Chapter Seven:
THE PATTERN

Getting Started

Does anyone in your group enjoy reading Christian biographies? If so, whose life story has been especially meaningful to you? What inspired you about that person's life?

Going Deeper

1. How is Jesus the perfect pattern of what it means to live a fully surrendered life:

- In His pre-incarnate existence (i.e., prior to coming to earth in human form)?
- In His incarnation (coming to earth)?
- In His wilderness temptation?
- In His earthly ministry?
- In Gethsemane?
- In His crucifixion?
- Throughout eternity?

2. For Jesus, surrender to God's will meant suffering at times. Why do you think Jesus was able, not only to *do* His Father's will, but to *delight* in doing the will of God? How can we learn to *delight* to obey God?

3. Describe a recent occasion when your natural desires were contrary to the will of God, and you chose to *bow the head* in surrender to the will of God.

4. What is an issue you are currently facing in which you need to *bow your head?* Pray for each other in relation to those needed points of surrender.

For Next Time

Throughout the week ahead, ask God to make you alert to opportunities to bow your head in submission to His will.

Grace Note

Jesus' surrender to His Father's will spans from eternity past, through His earthly life and ministry, and continues all the way to Calvary and beyond for all eternity. Though we as redeemed sinners will fail many tests on this earth, we have a Savior who stands at the right hand of the Father interceding for us at this moment and every time we are tempted to resist the will of God. Put your trust in His triumphs on your behalf as you bow your head in glad surrender to His loving control.

Chapter Eight:
YES, LORD!

Getting Started

Can you think of a time when you surrendered to God by faith, contrary to your feelings, and some time later, God allowed you to see the positive results of that choice—either in your life or someone else's life?

Giving Thanks!

Undoubtedly you have some specific testimonies of the Holy Spirit's work among the members of your group as a result of this study—beyond what may already have been shared in previous meetings. Provide an opportunity for each individual to express gratitude for what God has done during your time together. You may want to share about:

- A change in your thinking about—or your heart attitude toward—the will of God

- An area of your life where you were resisting God but have now surrendered to His control

• One or more areas of your life where you have been challenged to say, *Yes, Lord!*

• A specific passage of Scripture God has used to bring you to a place of greater surrender

• The ways the bad fruit of tyranny has been replaced by the good fruit of trust

• The prayer you wrote out as a "contract" with the Lord

• Any new insights into the character, heart, and ways of God

A Final Project

Think of one or more individuals whose walk with God has inspired you to a life of greater surrender. Write a note to one or more of those people. Share what you have observed in their lives and how their surrender to God has influenced your life. Remember the encouragement from Proverbs 11:25: "The generous soul will be made rich, and he who waters will also be watered himself."

Revive Our Hearts™

Offering sound, biblical teaching and encouragement for women through . . .

 Books & Resources Nancy's books, True Woman books, and a wide range of audio/video

 Broadcasting Two daily, nationally syndicated broadcasts (Revive Our Hearts and Seeking Him with Nancy Leigh DeMoss) reaching some one million listeners a week

 Events & Training True Woman Conferences and events designed to equip women's ministry leaders and pastors' wives

 Internet ReviveOurHearts.com, TrueWoman.com, LiesYoungWomenBelieve.com, daily blogs, and a large, searchable collection of electronic resources for women in every season of life

Believing God for a grassroots movement of authentic revival and biblical womanhood . . .
Encouraging women to:

- Discover and embrace God's design and mission for their lives
- Reflect the beauty and heart of Jesus Christ to their world
- Intentionally pass on the baton of Truth to the next generation
- Pray earnestly for an outpouring of God's Spirit in their families, churches, nation, and world

Visit us at **ReviveOurHearts.com**. We'd love to hear from you!

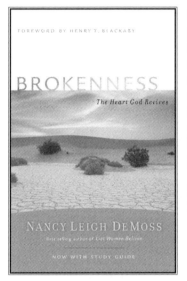

Do you need a fresh infusion of the grace of God in your life? *Brokenness* is an invitation to encounter God in a whole new way. It is a call to discover His heart and His ways; a challenge to embrace a radically new way of thinking and living, in which the way up is down, death brings life, and brokenness is the pathway to wholeness.

Brokenness
ISBN-13: 978-0-8024-1281-2

Your fullest experience of God will only come when your life is holy and your heart is pure. If you're longing for a deeper connection with God, you must first answer His call to holiness. Here Nancy Leigh DeMoss shares practical principles for having a life that is set apart and a heart that is set on fire.

Holiness
ISBN13: 978-0-8024-1279-9